THE GREAT REBALANCING

THE GREAT REBALANCING

Trade, Conflict, and the Perilous Road Ahead
for the World Economy

MICHAEL PETTIS

with a new preface by the author

PRINCETON UNIVERSITY PRESS
Princeton and Oxford

Copyright © 2013 by Princeton University Press
Published by Princeton University Press, 41 William Street, Princeton, New Jersey 08540
In the United Kingdom: Princeton University Press, 6 Oxford Street, Woodstock, Oxfordshire OX20 1TW

press.princeton.edu

Sixth printing, and first paperback printing, with a new preface by the author, 2014

Paperback ISBN: 978-0-691-16362-8

The Library of Congress has cataloged the cloth edition of this book as follows

Pettis, Michael.
   The great rebalancing : trade, conflict, and the perilous road ahead for the world economy /
Michael Pettis.
      p.   cm.
   Includes bibliographical references and index.
   ISBN 978-0-691-15868-6 (hbk.)
   1. Balance of trade.   2. Balance of payments.   3. International trade.   4. International
economic relations.   5. Financial crises.   I. Title.

HF1014.P46 2013
3829.17—dc23   2012039175

British Library Cataloging-in-Publication Data is available

This book has been composed in Minion Pro, Futura, and ITC Mona Lisa Std

Printed on acid-free paper.

Printed in the United States of America

7 9 10 8 6

To my mom, from whom most of my very few good habits come, and to my friends Zhang Gengwang, Charles Saliba, and the brilliant former and current students of my central bank seminar at Peking University, who have helped make my ten years in China (and counting) a real pleasure.

"But I don't want to go among mad people," said Alice. "Oh, you can't help that," said the Cat. "We're all mad here."

—Lewis Carroll

The exportation of our moneys in trade of merchandize is a means to increase our treasure.

—Tomas Mun of London, merchant, 1664

The crisis takes a much longer time coming than you think, and then it happens much faster than you would have thought.

—Rudiger Dornbusch

CONTENTS

PREFACE TO THE PAPERBACK EDITION

WHEN I WROTE THIS BOOK NEARLY two years ago my goal was to work out the underlying imbalances that explained the sources of growth in the global economy, especially before the 2007–08 crisis, and why the subsequent adjustment was inevitably going to be difficult. The world economy was characterized, I argued, by significant savings imbalances, and it was important to see the current crisis within its historical context. Savings imbalances have preceded many, if not most, of the global crises of the past 200 years—to the extent that Karl Marx even placed this process at the center of his argument as to why the demise of capitalism was inevitable.

Has the world changed much since I wrote this book? In fact it seems to be following the script fairly closely, although we still have a long way to go before we can declare the current global crisis over, and indeed in some parts of the developing world the impact of the crisis has only just started to become apparent. As I expected, and as my model suggested, the U.S. has been the first major economy to adjust, and although its recovery is still fragile and can easily be derailed, mainly by events in Europe, it seems pretty safe to bet that the U.S. will continue to lead the slow, painful path towards a global rebalancing.

It will not be easy. China has finally begun its long-awaited rebalancing and growth rates have dropped sharply. It has, in other words, begun to reverse the domestic imbalances it had built up especially over the previous decade. The process, however, is far from over. As of this writing President Xi Jinping has moved strongly to consolidate power and it is only if he is successful that Beijing will be able to impose the difficult reforms that will transform the economy at the expense, and with their tremendous resistance, of the very elite that had benefitted disproportionately from thirty years of miraculous growth.

The consensus for Chinese GDP growth in 2014 and 2015 is that it will come very close to the 7.5 percent target proposed by Beijing, but I expect actual growth will be lower. Beijing must rein in credit growth, but policymakers cannot do so without GDP growth rates falling substantially from current levels. The longer they take, the greater the risk that we reach debt capacity constraints, in which case China faces a possible collapse in growth.

As of now, however, I do not expect this to happen. I believe that the new leadership in Beijing understands how urgent it is to rebalance the economy, and so rather than a collapse in growth, I expect GDP growth rates will continue to drop by 1–2 percentage points every year during the rest of this decade. In chapter 4 of this book I argued that the upper limit of GDP growth on average during the 2013–23 period under President Xi and his administration is likely to be 3–4 percent. As surprising as this prediction might seem (and it seemed even more surprising two years ago), it follows almost inevitably from my explanation of the Chinese growth model, and I have no reason to modify my claim.

For the reasons discussed in this book I continue to be more pessimistic about the outlook for Europe. The peripheral countries of Europe have managed to roll over their debts thanks to aggressive easing by the European Central Bank. This is not, however, a solution to Europe's economic crisis. It would only be a solution if Europe's problem were mainly a short-term liquidity problem.

It isn't. For many of the highly indebted countries of peripheral Europe, debt levels are unsustainably high and continue to rise much faster than GDP. It will take a near-infinite commitment by Germany to prevent an eventual default or restructuring. This can go on for several more years, of course, and because German banks are insufficiently capitalized to recognize potential losses, Berlin will want urgently to roll over the debt until German banks have rebuilt their capital base. Once Berlin is no longer able to increase its exposure, however, or once the German electorate revolts, that commitment will end and the creditors of much of peripheral Europe will be forced into granting implicit or explicit debt forgiveness.

Meanwhile the very important reforms that are taking place, especially in the labor markets of countries like Spain, will do little to address the underlying European problems. There is too much debt and too little domestic demand, largely because, as I show in chapter 6, domestic demand was suppressed by policies in Germany at the turn of the century aimed at forcing down workers' wages.

The austerity policies aimed at addressing the debt burden are, in a horrible irony, reducing demand further and, with it, worsening the economic crisis. In a world of excess capacity, without more demand there can be no growth, and without growth it will be impossible for peripheral Europe to service debt without German help. The debt may be rolled forward another two or three years, but eventually a substantial portion will be written off, either explicitly or implicitly, and only after this occurs will peripheral Europe return to growth.

As I argued in the last chapter of this book, one way or the other the world must rebalance and it will, and so far it is doing so almost exactly according to script. Major imbalances are unsustainable and always eventually reverse, but there are worse ways and better ways they can do so. The fundamental problem, as I see it, is that until the underlying structural tendencies to force up the savings rates in certain parts of the world are reversed, we will not arrive at any real equilibrium that does not involve high levels of global unemployment for many more years.

One of the things I did not do in this book, and many readers subsequently pointed it out and asked me to redress it, was to explain why this structural tendency to distort the global savings rates existed in the first place. There is nothing new about distortions in the savings rates. We have seen these kinds of imbalances many times before, for example in the 1960s and early 1970s with the surge in OPEC revenues, and in the 1920s with rampant income inequality. In both cases these periods of distorted global savings were followed by global imbalances, surging debt, and, finally, economic crises.

For this reason I have added to this edition of my book a substantial appendix in which I show why two important trends—rising income inequality throughout the world and consumption-repressing policies, especially in Germany and China—necessarily had to lead in the short-term to excess credit-fueled consumption in some countries and an explosion in speculative and ultimately non-productive investment everywhere. In the appendix I show that because neither of these responses were sustainable, it was inevitable that the developed world would experience a surge in global unemployment once debt levels became too high. This was an automatic consequence of rising income inequality.

For new readers of my book I would suggest that it might be more useful to read the appendix first before reading the book. In the appendix I show why the combination of income inequality and consumption repression must lead inexorably to the kinds of imbalances that we have seen in the world over the past two decades. It is these imbalances that drive much of what I discuss in this book.

THE GREAT REBALANCING

CHAPTER ONE

Trade Imbalances and the Global Financial Crisis

The source of the global crisis through which we are living can be found in the great trade and capital flow imbalances of the past decade or two. Unfortunately because balance of payments mechanisms are so poorly understood, much of the debate about the crisis is caught up in muddled analysis.

EVER SINCE THE U.S. SUBPRIME CRISIS began in 2007–8, caused in large part by an uncontrolled real estate boom and consumption binge, fueled in both cases by overly abundant capital and low interest rates, the world has been struggling with a series of deep and seemingly unrelated financial and economic crises. The most notable of these is the crisis affecting Europe, which deepened spectacularly in 2010–11.

For reasons we will see in chapter 6, Europe's crisis will probably lead to a partial breakup of the euro as well as to defaults or debt restructurings among one or more European sovereign borrowers. The only things likely to save the euro—fiscal union or, as I discuss in chapter 6, a major reversal of German trade imbalances—seem politically improbable as of the time of this writing.

But it is not the just the United States and Europe that have been affected. The global crisis has also accelerated pressure on what was already going to be a very difficult transition for China from an extremely imbalanced growth model to something more sustainable over the long term. For political reasons the adjustment had to be postponed through 2012 because of the leadership transition and the need to develop a consensus, but the longer the postponement the more difficult the transition will be.

The events surrounding the ouster from the Politburo in early 2012 of Bo Xilai, the former mayor of Chongqing, show just how difficult the impact of the transition is likely to be on the political elite, who have benefitted most from the existing growth model. But as difficult as it will undoubtedly be, one way or another, for reasons that will be explained in this book, China must make the transition. As a consensus about the need for a radical transformation of the growth model develops, and China begins adjusting over the next two or three years, the impact of the global crisis will probably manifest itself in the form of a "lost" decade or longer for China of much slower growth and soaring government debt.

What's more, a Chinese adjustment will necessarily bring with it adverse and perhaps even destabilizing shocks to developing countries heavily reliant on the export of commodities, especially nonfood commodities. Countries as far apart as Brazil and Australia, that have bet heavily on continued growth in China and the developed world, will be sharply affected when Chinese investment growth, which was ramped up dramatically in 2009 and 2010 after the United States and Europe faltered (and so more than compensated for the initial impact on commodity prices of reduced American and European demand), itself begins to falter. The crisis that began in the United States, in other words, has or will adversely affect the whole world, although not at the same time.

But for all their complex global impact, it is worth pointing out that from a historical point of view there is nothing mysterious about the various crises and their interconnections. For almost any serious student of financial and economic history, what has happened in the past few years as the world adjusts to deep imbalances is neither unprecedented nor should have even been unexpected. The global crisis is a financial crisis driven primarily by global trade and capital imbalances, and it has unfolded in almost a textbook fashion.

There is nonetheless a tendency, especially among Continental European policymakers and the nonspecialized Western media, to see the crisis as caused by either the systematic deregulation of the financial services industry or the use and abuse of derivatives. When this crisis is viewed, however, from a historical perspective it is almost impossible to agree with either of these claims. There have been after all many well-recorded financial crises in history, dating at least from the Roman real estate crisis of AD 33, which shared many if not most characteristics of the 2007 crisis.

Earlier crises occurred among financial systems under very different regulatory regimes, some less constrained and others more constrained, and in which the use of derivatives was extremely limited or even nonexistent. It is hard to see why we would explain the current crisis in a way that could not also serve as an explanation for earlier crises. Perhaps it is just easier to focus on easily understandable deficiencies. As Hyman Minsky explained,

> Once the sharp financial reaction occurs, institutional deficiencies will be evident. Thus, after a crisis, it will always be possible to construct plausible arguments—by emphasizing the trigger events or institutional flaws—that accidents, mistakes, or easily correctible shortcomings were responsible for the disaster.[1]

Minsky went on to argue that these "plausible" arguments miss the point. Financial instability has to do with underlying monetary and balance sheet conditions, and when these conditions exist, any financial system will tend toward instability—in fact periods of financial stability, Minsky argued, will themselves change financial behavior in ways that cause destabilizing shifts and that increase the subsequent risk of crisis.

Why do underlying monetary conditions become destabilizing? Charles Kindleberger suggested that there are many different sources of monetary shock, from gold discoveries, to financial innovation, to capital recycling, that can lead eventually to instability,[2] but the classic explanation of the origins of crises in capitalist systems, one followed by Marxist as well as many non-Marxist economists, points to imbalances between production and consumption in the major economies as the primary source of monetary instability.

Underconsumption

According to this view growing income inequality and wealth concentration leave household consumers unable to absorb all that is produced within the economy. One of the consequences is that as surplus savings (savings are simply the difference between total production and total consumption) grow to unsustainable levels, and because declining consumption undermines the rationale for investing in order to expand productive facilities, these excess savings are increasingly directed into speculative investments or are exported abroad.

Most economists, including Marxists, have tended to see these imbalances between production and consumption as occurring and getting resolved within a single country, but in fact imbalances in one country can force obverse imbalances in other countries through the trade account. In the late nineteenth century economists like the Englishman John Hobson and the American Charles Arthur Conant, both scandalously underrated by economists today, explained how the process works. Although neither was a Marxist, it is worth noticing that Hobson did heavily influence Lenin's theory of imperialism, and this influence was felt all the way to the Latin American *dependencia* theorists of the 1960s and 1970s.

Hobson and Conant argued that the leading capitalist economies turned to imperialism primarily in order to export surplus savings and import foreign demand as a way of addressing the domestic savings imbalances. This has become widely accepted among economic historians—Niall Ferguson wrote pithily in his biography of Siegmund Warburg, for example, that "late 19th Century imperialism rested above all on capital exports."[3] So, perhaps, does its modern equivalent. As Charles Arthur Conant put it in 1900,

> For many years there was an outlet at a high rate of return for all the savings of all the frugal persons in the great civilized countries. Frightful miscalculations were made and great losses incurred, because experience had not gauged the value or the need of new works under all conditions, but there was room for the legitimate use of all savings without loss, and in the enterprises affording an adequate return.

The conditions of the early part of the century have changed. Capital is no longer needed in the excess of the supply, but it is becoming congested. The benefits of savings have been inculcated with such effect for many decades that savings accumulate beyond new demands for capital which are legitimate, and are becoming a menace to the economic future of the great industrial countries.[4]

Conant went on to say that as we consumed ever smaller shares of what we produced—perhaps because the wealthy captured an increasing share of income and their consumption did not rise with their wealth—domestic savings eventually exceeded the ability for domestic investment to serve "legitimate" needs, which was to expand domestic capacity and infrastructure to meet domestic consumption. This happened at least in part because the excess savings themselves reduced domestic consumption, and so reduced the need to expand domestic production facilities. When this happened the major industrialized nations had to turn abroad. In that case these countries exported their excess savings, thereby importing foreign demand for domestic production.

Like in the past two decades, this need to export savings was at the heart of trade and capital flow imbalances during the last few decades of the nineteenth century and the first few decades of the twentieth century. It was however the most industrialized countries that were the source of excess savings in Conant's day, whereas today the major exporters of excess savings range from rich countries like Germany and Japan to very poor countries like China.

In a 2011 article Kenneth Austin, an international economist with the U.S. Treasury Department, made explicit the comparison between the two periods. He wrote, speaking of the earlier version,

The basic idea is that oversaving causes insufficient demand for economic output. In turn, that leads to recession and resource misallocation, including excessive investment in marketing and distribution. This was a direct challenge to a core thesis of the classical economists: "Savings are always beneficial because they allow greater accumulation of capital."

 . . . . Hobson took his excess savings theory in another direction in *Imperialism: A Study*, first published in 1902. In a closed economy, excess savings cause recessions, but an open economy has another alternative: domestic savers can invest abroad. Hobson attributed the renewed enthusiasm for colonial conquest among the industrial powers of the day to a need to find new foreign markets and investment opportunities. He called this need to vent the excess savings abroad "The Economic Taproot of Imperialism."

However, increasing foreign investment requires earning the necessary foreign exchange to invest abroad. This requires an increase in net exports. So foreign investment solves two problems at once. It reduces the excess supply of goods and drains the pool of excess saving. The two objectives are simultaneously fulfilled because they are, in fact and theory, logically equivalent.[5]

When domestic consumption has been insufficient to justify enough domestic investment to absorb the high savings that were themselves the result of low consumption—usually because the working and middle classes had too small a share of total income, and we will see in chapter 4 how this happened in China—countries have historically exported capital as a way of absorbing foreign consumption. With the exporting of these excess savings, and the concomitant importing of foreign demand, international trade and capital flows necessarily resulted in deep imbalances.

The Different Explanations of Trade Imbalance

This argument, which we can call the "underconsumptionist" argument, is of course not the only theory that explains trade imbalances. There are at least two other theories of trade imbalance that share a number of features but are fundamentally different.

The most common explanation for trade imbalances is "mercantilism." Broadly speaking mercantilist countries put into place policies, including most commonly import restraints and export subsidies, aimed at generating a positive balance of trade in which the country exports more than it imports.

The defense of mercantilism is that it permits the practitioner to generate net inflows of assets that can be accumulated for a number of purposes.

It isn't always clear exactly what these purposes are, but the main justification, historically, seems to have been the ability to wage war. During the classic mercantilist age a positive balance of trade resulted in the accumulation of gold and silver, and this hoard of treasure assured the monarch of the ability to hire soldiers and sailors, pay for armaments, and afford costly foreign engagements.

Today, of course, countries are more likely to accumulate assets mainly in the form of foreign exchange reserves at the central bank or in the form of private ownership of foreign assets. The hoard of central bank reserves is driven not so much by military needs as by the need to defend the stability of the currency, maintain payments on foreign loans and obligations, and, most important, guarantee access to imported commodities in times of financial stress.

Although countries like China, Japan, Korea, and Germany have been accused of mercantilism for many years, this particular charge isn't really a satisfactory explanation of what they do and why. Clearly for a highly volatile developing country there are benefits to accumulating a certain amount of foreign reserves. This cannot be the whole explanation, however. Given how domestic monetary policies are distorted by the accumulation of reserves, it is hard to explain why rich countries employ mercantilist policies, or why poor countries like China accumulate levels of foreign exchange reserves that far exceed even the most generous estimate of what would be appropriate. In either case mercantilism simply does not make sense.

A better explanation of what they do, interestingly enough, may be found in what many consider to be one of the classic documents of mercantilism, Thomas Mun's *England's Treasure by Foreign Trade*, published posthumously in 1664. In his tract, rather than encourage trade intervention simply for the sake of state accumulation of specie, he proposed a much more sophisticated argument, based not so much on direct intervention to achieve a positive trade balance but rather on measures to "soberly refrain from excessive consumption." For Mun, the accumulation of specie would lead to greater availability of capital domestically, and so would lower costs of capital for businesses. It was this lower cost of capital that would promote domestic economic growth.

With this argument we are back, it seems, to a version of John Hobson's underconsumptionist argument. Although Mun didn't state this explicitly, what we often think of as trade intervention, as I will show in chapters 2 and 3, is often just policies that effectively force up a country's savings rate by transferring income from household consumers to the tradable goods sector, thereby creating a gap between GDP growth and consumption growth. By forcing up the savings rate through consumption-constraining policies, these policies lower the domestic cost of capital and encourage investment.

We will come back to this several times over the next few chapters, but it is worth mentioning that countries like China, Japan before 1990, South Korea, and other Asian Tigers are, properly speaking, neither mercantilist nor export driven. They are, as we will see in chapter 4 in the case of China, investment-driven economies. Their large trade surpluses were or are simply a necessary residual of policies that consciously or not forced up the savings rate to fund domestic investment. As I will also show, the subsequent imbalances that are created by structural constraints to consumption can become seriously destabilizing, both for the world and for the countries that employ these policies.

For the sake of completion we should mention that the third theory that justifies trade intervention is the "infant industry" argument, whose most brilliant exponent, and who probably first came up with the phrase, is the first American treasury secretary Alexander Hamilton. In his *Report on the Manufacturers to the U.S. Congress* in December 1791, Hamilton argued that it was in the best interests of the United States that certain industries be encouraged to develop quickly because the externalities (although of course he did not use this word) associated with these industries were significant:

> And if it may likewise be assumed as a fact that manufactures open a wider field to exertions of ingenuity than agriculture, it would not be a strained conjecture, that the labor employed in the former being at once more constant, more uniform and more ingenious, than that which is employed in the latter, will be found at the same time more productive.

The problem, according to Hamilton, was that because British and other European industrialists were so far advanced in terms of productivity and organization, Americans simply would not be able to compete for many years unless the government imposed tariffs on foreign-made goods. The goal of protection, in this case, was primarily to create enough space for American industrialists to catch up to Europeans. Once they did so, the tariffs could be removed.

Although the infant industry argument has been and still is used often to explain trade intervention, it is also an unsatisfactory explanation for current imbalances. Of the three largest surplus nations, two of them, Germany and Japan, can hardly be said to be technologically backward and in need of protection. The third, China, discourages the brutal domestic competition that is necessary to drive technological innovation and productivity growth behind protectionist barriers, so trade protection in China is unlikely to lead to rapid growth in innovation. It is at best an infant industry policy that strangles the infant by trying to create state-protected national champions.

Destabilizing Imbalances

We are left, as I will show, with underconsumption as the most likely cause of global trade distortions. Trade imbalances, of course, don't always lead to crisis. In any well-functioning global trading system there are always likely to be small and temporary imbalances in trade flows. In some cases, primarily in the case of countries in the midst of a long-term investment boom like the United States for much of the nineteenth century, trade imbalances can be sustainable and even persist for many years without necessarily leading to crisis. Even in the case of the United States in the nineteenth century, however, there were financial crises nearly every decade or so, some of which were linked to trade imbalances and others caused by the "frightful miscalculations" to which Charles Arthur Conant referred.

But even otherwise sustainable trade imbalances can lead to crisis when they create fragile national balance sheets. This can happen because trade flow imbalances, of course, require their obverse, capital flow imbalances, and capital flows can be and often are structured in ways that are instable and lead to fragility in national balance sheets.

Still, certain kinds of trade imbalances, driven primarily by high levels of investment in the trade deficit countries, need not be destabilizing. They can persist for many years, but eventually the system automatically adjusts when many years of productive investment begin to generate the rising production of goods and services and there is a reversal in these imbalances.

The reversal of the trade imbalances occurs as either the cause or the consequence of a reversal in capital flows. As I will explain later in this chapter, countries that repay foreign investment must run current account surpluses, just as countries that run current account surpluses must be net exporters of capital. In other cases, a country that runs trade deficits for many years not driven by surging domestic investment necessarily sees anyway a rise in foreign capital inflows (trade deficits must always be funded by foreign investment). In this case, however, the liabilities generated by the inflows are not associated with an increase in domestic asset growth, and so foreign obligations rise at an unsustainable pace.

At some point, perhaps after several years, domestic prices or the value of the trade deficit country's currency should adjust downward to the point at which there is a reversal of the trade deficit. It is only by running a trade surplus that a country can return the capital inflow that it previously imported.

So although trade imbalances can exist naturally, they eventually rebalance in an orderly way. But not all trade imbalances are natural. When imbalances that are not associated with a large increase in productive investment in the deficit country become large and persist for many years, it is almost always because policy distortions, or distortions in the institutional framework constraining or governing these trade flows, have prevented the adjustment from taking place. Large and persistent trade imbalances, in other words, are almost always caused by distortions in financial, industrial, or trade policies.

These distortions can prevent adjustments for many years, but large imbalances ultimately are unsustainable because the capital flows that finance the trade imbalances can be reversed only with a reversal of the trade imbalances. Eventually these imbalances will adjust in spite of policy and institutional constraints, but in this case the adjustment is often violent and can come in the form of a financial crisis. In that sense there is nothing unique, unexpected, or even surprising about the recent global crisis. It was simply the necessary and chaotic adjustment after many years of policy distortions that forced large and persistent capital imbalances.

The main imbalances of recent years were the very large trade surpluses during the past decade of China, Germany, and Japan and the very large trade deficits of the United States and peripheral Europe. There are many precedents to the global crisis through which we are living. In fact many, if not most, of the global and regional crises that preceded it during the past two hundred years were driven by the same kinds of imbalances, most famously the global crisis in the 1930s and the so-called LDC (less developed countries) crisis in the 1980s.

So none of what is happening today is new, but what is often forgotten is that policies in the country or countries that first suffered from the crises—usually the trade deficit countries—have not always, and perhaps not even usually, caused the distortions. It is important to recognize that these imbalances had their roots in policy distortions in both the countries that ran large trade deficits and those that ran large trade surpluses. For the former, the large deficits led to unsustainable increases in debt and, ultimately, to the deleveraging process necessary to restore balance. It is this deleveraging process that is at the heart of the global financial crisis.

We Have the Tools

The crisis will not be truly over until the policies and institutional framework that led to the large trade imbalances have been sufficiently modified. And yet it seems that few aspects of the political and economic debate surrounding the resolution of the various crises are as confused as our understanding of the balance of payments mechanisms that govern trade and capital flows. As a result, much of the debate on what to do and how to avoid similar crises in the future is muddled and usually misses the point.

This, however, is not because we do not have adequate tools with which to understand the functioning of the global balance of payments. On the contrary, the basic economic principles underlying international trade and capital flows are fairly well understood, but they are at times so counterintuitive that even economists who should know better are seduced into saying things that make no sense.

We know for example the relationship among savings, investment, and current account imbalances in any particular country, but we fail to apply this knowledge logically to the full range of policies and institutions that affect the components of the global trade and capital balances. We fail to think in terms of the overall system. In this book, it turns out, we will not need to learn any new economic theory.

What is new about this book is that in it I extend our basic knowledge of open economies and apply it to the global economy as a single closed system in order to show the many surprising ways policies and conditions are related. Japanese interest rates, Spanish real estate bubbles, American mortgage derivatives, and copper mining in Chile are all part of a single system in which distortions in any one part must have automatic consequences for all the others. Financiers in São Paulo earn substantially higher compensation than their peers in London in part because Chinese households receive an artificially low return on their deposits. There are huge tracts of empty homes outside of Dublin in part because of the overvaluation of East Germany's currency after reunification.

The global system, in other words, is a system in which every part is affected by every other part through the capital and current accounts. For example, we often hear that the current account deficits of peripheral Europe and the United States have little to do with German or Chinese policies but are rather primarily the consequence of the very low savings rates in the deficit countries. It turns out that this widely repeated claim, which even has an attractive ring of old-fashioned morality about it, is nearly meaningless, as I will show in chapters 2 and 3 of this book. Current account deficits are by definition equal to the gap between savings and investment, but they are rarely "caused" by too little savings except as a tautology.

More important, the savings rate and savings level of any country are determined largely not by the thriftiness of its citizen but by policies at home and among trade partners. To say therefore that the crisis in Spain, for example, is caused by the spendthrift habits of Spanish citizens relative to the thriftiness and hard work of their German cousins is to misunderstand altogether the root causes of the European crisis and to replace an understanding of the formal working of the global trading system with cheap and empty moralizing. We will see why in chapter 6.

And yet these kinds of almost nonsensical claims appeal to many of us— especially, it seems, if we are wealthy financiers. Perhaps it is because they allow us to make easy distinctions between moral and immoral economic behavior, even if these distinctions are wrong. To the extent that they affect policy, unfortunately, they actually retard the global recovery.

If we misunderstand the root causes of the global imbalances that led to the global crisis, then it is unlikely that we will choose optimal policies that will allow us to work our way out of the imbalances in the least painful way possible. On the contrary, as John Maynard Keynes so urgently argued nearly eighty years ago, we are likely to choose policies that maximize global unemployment and lead directly to trade conflict. This is almost certainly happening again as surplus countries insist that the bulk of the global adjustment take place in the form of austerity in the deficit countries. Deficit country austerity may indeed be part of the correct prescription, but if it is not more than fully matched with surplus-country reflation, it cannot possibly succeed without a sharp rise in global unemployment.

We can see the consequences of our muddled thinking most strikingly in the European crisis. Thanks to a general inability to understand why the advent of the euro spelled trouble for much of peripheral Europe, the policies needed to save the euro are largely ignored. What is worse, only Germany can save the euro, but this will require a dramatic, and improbable, shift in Berlin's understanding of the root causes of the crisis.

Saving the euro will not require that Berlin make funding more easily available for peripheral Europe, as too many policymakers believe. Nor will the euro be helped if foreign central banks, including China's, buy more

European government debt. The euro can survive only if Berlin reverses policies that forced German savings to grow at the expense of households, thus forcing down savings rates in peripheral Europe to dangerous levels and dooming the euro. German policymakers refuse to take the necessary steps because they refuse to pay the cost of the adjustment.

It is not hard to understand why Germans are reluctant to take the necessary steps because these must lead to rising debt and slower growth in Germany, but it should also be clear that if Germany does not do so, there is no reason to expect a "solution" to the euro crisis. This is why the euro experiment will almost certainly fail and Germany will suffer anyway from rising debt and slowing growth. We will see why in chapter 6.

It is worth pointing out however that no matter how wrongheaded current policies are, Europe, like the rest of the world, will adjust from its trade imbalances one way or the other. It has no choice. But if Europe rebalances in a suboptimal way—that is, without a policy reversal in Germany—its rebalancing will ultimately become far more costly for Germany than a reversal of policies today, as I will explain in this book. We saw the same thing happen in the late 1920s, when the United States refused to reflate domestic demand sufficiently to rebalance global trade. When trade rebalanced anyway, as it always must, the United States was among those that suffered most.

Why the Confusion?

As I see it there are three very large areas of confusion and muddled thinking when it comes to discussing trade and global imbalances. The first area has to do with the causes of significant trade imbalances. Although in a well-managed global economy with few distortions and flexible financial systems there are always likely to be countries with current account surpluses and deficits, in fact it is worth repeating that very large persistent surpluses and deficits are almost always the result of distorted policies in one or more countries.

There are many ways in which these distortions can occur. It is easy to think of trade tariffs and currency manipulation as forms of trade intervention, but I will argue in chapters 2 and 3 that although they certainly do cause distortions in trade, they do not do so for the reasons we generally assume. Their impact on trade is not directly though relative price changes but rather indirectly by changing the relationship between consumption and GDP.

By understanding how and why they actually cause trade distortions, we can understand more generally how a whole range of industrial, tax, and financial policies that seem unrelated to trade can, in fact, cause significant trade distortions. We will also see how these distortions have their counterpart in the fragility of national balances sheets that build up around these distortions.

The second large area of confusion and muddled thinking has to do with the relationship among trade, the savings rate, and international capital flows. The three are linked, of course, but the way they are linked is more complex and subtle than most analysts recognize. Policies that affect trade balances usually do so by affecting the savings and investment rates, both at home and abroad, and changes in the savings and investment rates automatically affect capital flows.

It is important to understand these relationships in order to understand how policies in one country can force corresponding changes in another country, and it is important to understand that the savings rate is not an independent variable that can be altered at will, or with the right moralistic exhortations. If it is to be altered in an orderly way, it can be done only with changes in the underlying policies both at home and abroad that led to excessively high or low savings rates in different countries. Otherwise the savings rate will ultimately adjust anyway, but it will do so in a disorderly way, with abrupt disruptions to international trade.

The third area of confusion has to do with the role of the U.S. dollar as the global reserve currency and with the role of central bank reserves more generally. There is a tendency to believe that global trade is denominated primarily in U.S. dollars because of sinister or not-so-sinister designs of the U.S. government, and that countries are forced to accumulate U.S. dollars if they want to accumulate foreign currency reserves.

It is also widely believed that the use of the U.S. dollar as the global reserve currency confers upon the United States enormous advantages. This has been referred to as the exorbitant privilege of the U.S. dollar.

In fact I will show in chapters 7 and 8 that reserve currency denomination has little to do with U.S. power or dominance and much more to do with trade policy in foreign countries and an accommodating financial and monetary system in the United States. The astonishing accumulation of dollar reserves in the past decade was the consequence—sometimes intended and sometimes unintended—of a wide range of policies aimed at generating growth in those countries, and these are inextricably linked to the causes of the global crisis.

And contrary to popular belief, it is not in the interest of the United States that countries continue to accumulate mostly dollars in their central bank reserves. In fact I will argue that excessive use of the U.S. dollar internationally actually forces up either American debt or American unemployment. It is more of a burden for the United States than a privilege.

For that reason it is actually in the best interest of the United States—although perhaps against the best short-term interest of China and other countries that seek to grow rapidly—that the U.S. government place restrictions on the ability of foreign countries to hold U.S. dollar reserves. This will both benefit the American economy and stabilize the global environment.

This book is broadly divided into three sections that mirror and address these three areas of confusion. In the second and third chapters of this book I discuss the issue of trade intervention—or more specifically what kinds of policies affect a country's trade balance—and how policies that may or may not have directly to do with trade intervention in one country may in fact affect that country's trade balance. In the fourth chapter I focus on the case of China as an illustrative example of the various policies aimed at generating growth but one of whose results is necessarily upward pressure on domestic savings and the trade surplus.

In the next three chapters I address the international links among trade, capital flows, and savings. Chapter 5 shows how domestic policies that affect the ratio between savings and investment in one country must automatically affect the ratio between savings and investment in the rest of the world. Chapter 6 applies the analysis to the European crisis, and chapter 7 discusses the relationship among trade, savings, and international capital flows, and how central bank reserves function within the global trading system.

In chapter 8 I address the role of the dollar as the global reserve currency. In it I argue that the U.S. dollar's role as the global reserve currency places more of an exorbitant burden on the United States than an exorbitant privilege. And finally in the last chapter I discuss how global imbalances may eventually adjust and what the consequences will be.

Some Accounting Identities

Before going on to a more detailed discussion, it is useful to remember that every country's current account surplus is by definition equal to the excess of domestic savings over domestic investment. If a country saves more than it invests domestically, these excess savings must be invested abroad, and one of the automatic consequences of net foreign investment is an excess of exports over imports. Every country that has net investment abroad (i.e., it invests abroad more than foreigners invest domestically) must generate more revenues from the export of goods and services and from foreign interest and royalty payments than it pays out.

This simple fact, known as an accounting identity, goes a long way toward illuminating trade imbalances. In fact just three accounting identities—which are true by definition and so never can be violated—are enough to make sense of what otherwise seems like an incredibly complex phenomena. These are the following:

1. For every country, the current account and the capital account must balance to zero.[6] To put it another way, every dollar that enters a country, either in payment for that country's exports, in the form of royalty or services receipts, or in the form of foreign investment in domestic assets, must leave that country, either in payment for imports, in the form of royalty or services expenditures, or in the form of outward investment.

Why? Because if an economic entity in any country other than the United States is in possession of an American dollar, earned either by selling an asset to an American or exporting goods to an American, either it will use that dollar to purchase something from abroad or to make a foreign payment, or it will save the dollar by purchasing a U.S. asset. There is nothing else it can do with the dollar (even burning the dollar bill or leaving it forgotten in some drawer, it turns out, does not violate this rule). One way or the other the dollar must leave the country through the current or capital account, so the sum of dollars entering the country and dollars leaving the country is always equal to zero. Of course we use the U.S. dollar here for simplification, but it is true of any currency other than that of the referent county.

2.   For every country, the difference between total domestic savings and total domestic investment is equal to the net amount of capital imported or exported, and so is also equal to the current account surplus or deficit. This follows from the above. If in any country domestic savings exceed domestic investment, for example, the excess must be invested abroad.

This means the excess savings must be exported. By exporting capital abroad, that country must "import" it back in the form of a current account surplus. This is a very important point to which we will return again and again—there is effectively no difference between exporting capital and importing demand given that a country that exports capital abroad on a net basis must run a current account surplus.

3.   Everything that a country produces must be either consumed or saved (and "consumption" includes even assets or resources that are thrown away or otherwise wasted). Because the total of goods and services that a country produces is generally defined as its gross domestic product, or GDP, then a country's savings can be defined simply as its GDP less total household and other consumption.

These accounting identities have interesting and important implications. For one, if everything a country produces it either consumes or it saves, and if the excess of domestic savings over domestic investment is equal to a country's current account surplus, then it also follows that everything a country produces it must consume domestically, invest domestically, or export.

This is reinforced by the commonsense notion that there are three sources of demand for domestic producers—domestic consumption, domestic investment, and net consumption and investment from abroad, that is, the current account surplus. These three sources of demand are what generate domestic growth. They are inextricably linked.

Another implication is that the savings rates of different countries are linked through the trade account. If any country takes steps to change the gap between its total domestic savings and its total domestic investment, then those steps must also affect its trade balance. Because a change in one country's trade balance must be matched with an opposite change in the trade balance of all other countries, there must also be an opposite and equal change in the gap between the total domestic savings of the rest of the world and the total domestic investment of the rest of the world.

To put it in an easier way to understand, if Japan forces up its total savings relative to its total investment, either the total savings of the rest of the world must decline or the total investment of the rest of the world must rise (or, of course, some combination of the two). This is because under these conditions Japan's current account surplus must rise, and so the current account deficit of the rest of the world must rise by exactly the same amount.

The Inanity of Moralizing

The fact that a change in the relationship between savings and investment in one country must force an obverse change in the relationship between savings and investment in another country is a very important point. A country whose policies cause a change in its savings or its investment will automatically force a change in its current account. Because a change in its current account must mirror the change in the current account of the rest of the world, this means that those policies must force a change in the total savings or total investment of the rest of the world.

In a globalized world, in other words, savings and investment rates are not set wholly or in some cases even primarily by domestic cultural preferences or by domestic policies. They are heavily affected by foreign policies through the trade account.

When moralizers laud the thrifty habits of Germans and criticize the spendthrift ways of Spaniards, in other words, they may be wholly missing the point. It is very possible that both German and Spanish savings rates are determined not by cultural preferences but by government policies in either Germany or Spain that have altered the domestic relationship between investment and savings. We discuss how this happens later in this book, mainly in the fifth, sixth, and seventh chapters, in order to understand how policies in one country can affect savings in another.

It is worth pointing out that this understanding may come with an unpleasant cost. It is often hard for analysts to look abroad for conditions that positively or negatively affect their home economy because they may be far more confident of their knowledge about local conditions than about foreign conditions. What's more, it is much easier and perhaps more enjoyable to analyze the imbalances facing the world by moralizing about the virtues of thrift and hard work and by making grand statements about the cultural determinants of success.

For example, if the European crisis was caused because Greeks and Italians aren't as thrifty and hardworking as Germans, then the solution to the crisis is simply an exhortation that Greek and Italians act more like Germans. Take away from the Italians and Greeks their good food, their sense of fashion, and their smiles, according to this way of thinking, and they, Europe, and the rest of the world will be much better off.

Similarly, how do we explain China's high trade surplus? China runs a trade surplus because, as nearly everyone knows, Chinese households value thrift and hard work more than their trade competitors. In fact more generally we are told, as Kishore Mahbubani, a Singaporean academic and one of the more excited proponents of Confucian values, put it in his book *Can Asians Think?*, countries with "Confucian" value systems include "attachment to the family as an institution, deference to societal interests, thrift, conservatism in social mores, respect for authority."[7]

Leave aside that these values are typical of many rural societies, Confucian or not, the reality is much more complicated. High Chinese savings, as we will show, are largely a consequence of domestic policies that constrain consumption, and have little to do with cultural values. Understanding this requires that we understand how domestic policies and the institutional framework that governs the economy affects savings and investment imbalances. Culture and individual preferences, unfortunately, matter a lot less than we think, even if they are much easier to understand and discuss.

In fact the very Confucian culture that is widely credited for having created the rapid growth and high trade surpluses of the East Asian countries, for example, was also credited, only fifty years ago, with Asia's persistent and seemingly intractable poverty. Confucians, as everybody knew in the 1950s and 1960s, and as more than two thousand years of Chinese legalist criticism confirmed, were unalterably lazy and incapable of thrift. As far back as the fifth century BC, critics bewailed the laziness and spendthrift ways of the Confucians. Philosopher Mozi, writing during the Warring States period, complained that the Confucian

> turns his back on what is basic by refusing to work, and contents himself with laziness and arrogance. . . . . In the summer he begs for grain, but once the harvest is in, he goes chasing after big funerals. All his children follow him to eat and drink their fill. If he can manage a few of these funerals, it will be enough to get by.

Even Singapore's former prime minister, Lee Kuan Yew, widely seen in recent years as the most vocal proponent of the impact of Confucian values in explaining high savings and rapid growth in Asia, did not at first disagree with Mozi. In an April 28, 1974, article in Singapore's *Strait Times*, he complained that Singapore's Chinese "spend freely and save less," which, he claimed, justified his policies to force them to save out of current income.

But how things have changed since then. After Asia started to grow rapidly in the 1970s, our understanding of the impact of Confucian culture on growth seems to have reversed itself quite astonishingly. Now Confucianism, with its supposed propensities toward thrift and hard work, is enough to explain Asian growth fully.

It is at best strange that only a few decades after we "knew" that Confucian culture condemned Asians to poverty, so many commentators can now point to Confucian culture as one of the primary factors that explain the Asian growth miracle. This makes no sense. Clearly Confucian values cannot explain either the tendency toward thrift or the love of consumption.

So what really explains the high German and Chinese savings rates and the low savings rates in the United States and peripheral Europe? In this book I argue that they are both necessarily caused by institutions and policy, whether these are policies and institutional frameworks in the deficit countries, policies and institutional frameworks in the surplus countries, or both.

What's more, exhortations that deficit countries become thriftier are not only useless in resolving the imbalances, but to the extent that they are acted upon, they are likely to worsen the impact of the crisis. Perhaps more surprising, as I show, if deficit countries do indeed become as thrifty as surplus countries, it will ultimately place the brunt of the adjustment on the surplus countries, whose virtues the deficit countries are supposed to imitate.

The New Economic Writing

In his 1868 paper to the Manchester Statistical Society, "On Credit Cycles and the Origin of Commercial Panics," the British economist John Mills (1821–96), no relation to his more famous namesake, wrote,

It is scarcely a matter for surprise, and still less for regret, that every commercial crisis occurring in this country is promptly followed by a literature of pamphlets, discussing the phenomena and their supposed causes, while they are yet a matter of painful interest to the public's mind.

Nothing, it seems, has changed in 150 years. Financial crises still prompt an outpouring of analysis, and the recent crisis has been no exception. Like every financial crisis in modern history, our most recent one has been accompanied and followed by an enormous amount of economic writing and debate seeking to understand and explain the causes of the crisis.

Thanks to the Internet and the popularity of blogs, much of the best writing and debate has taken place in the modern equivalent of the nineteenth century's pamphlets, broadsheets, and coffeehouse discussions—economic blogs. For many years the development and understanding of economic theory was blighted, if that's not too strong a word, by the domination of specialized academic journals that evaded the big, interesting questions in order to focus on topics that were too often either trivial or irrelevant.

In recent years, however, we have seen a great surge in creative thinking, and of course plenty of nonsense too, on the subject of economics. Much of this has been produced by academic and nonacademic writers, often with real-world knowledge and experience, writing not for academic specialists but for the intelligent public on publicly available blogs. This new way of discussing economics has, in my opinion, been an unalloyed blessing for the development of economic knowledge and understanding. As the creator of one such blog, *China Financial Markets*, and as the follower and reader of many, I very much wanted to exploit the new mode of economic writing by writing this book in the spirit of the new economic blogs.

By this I mean that I do not intend to address my book primarily to academic specialists. The global balance of payments is not a branch of advanced mathematics. It can be fully discussed and explained with relatively simple models and logical concepts, just as it was by David Ricardo, Adam Smith, John Maynard Keynes, Ludwig von Mises, Irving Fisher, and other great economists in history.

What was good enough for them should be good enough for the rest of us. In this book I discuss trade and capital flows in a way that will, I hope, make sense to anyone else interested in understanding the mechanics of international trade and some of the factors that affect it.

The key I think is to understand the basic concepts that drive overall demand and supply for consumption and for investment, and to work logically through their consequences. Among other things I show in this book that attempts to isolate very narrowly defined factors that might affect trade balances and, using complex statistical analyses, to draw conclusions about their causal relations may be self-defeating because of the wide range of factors that affect trade balances and their often complex feedback relationships.

To take one example, numerous studies have been done to determine the causal relationship between currency intervention and trade. Some studies have found that countries that revalue their currencies see their trade surpluses decline while others have found that currency revaluation actually seems to lead to increases in the trade surplus. The mixed conclusions lead some to question whether or not there is any predictable relationship between the foreign exchange value of a country's currency and its trade balance.

Once we understand the relationship between the level of the currency and the trade balance, it should become perfectly obvious that currency revaluation cannot help but reduce the trade surplus because of its corresponding impact on the gap between domestic savings and investment. But what about those studies that "prove" that in some cases, like Japan after 1985 or China after 2005, a revaluing currency is associated with an *increase* in the trade surplus? Don't they prove that there is no clear causal relationship between currency policies and the trade balance?

No, they do not. They prove only that the level of the currency is not the only thing that affects the trade balance. If policymakers revalue their currency and then, because of concerns about the growth impact of revaluation, put into place other policies that try to limit the adverse growth impact in the short term of a currency revaluation, it is very possible that the net effect of those other policies on the trade balance overwhelms the impact of revaluation.

In that case it is perfectly possible that a currency revaluation "results" in a higher, not lower, trade surplus. In this case the revaluation led automatically to other policies—perhaps a rapid expansion of credit and a reduction of interest rates—that forced up the current account surplus by more than the revaluation forced it down.

Few nonexperts doubt that the level of the currency matters to the trade balance, and that revaluation tends to reduce the trade surplus. It takes a trained economist to propose the opposite. But I am convinced that if economists worked through the "big picture" of what affects a country's trade balance it will be almost impossible for them to doubt that currency revaluation, except in very special—and highly unlikely—circumstances, must increase imports relative to exports. In the next chapter I will try to explain why.

CHAPTER TWO

How Does Trade Intervention Work?

*It is widely understood that countries can intervene in trade
by imposing import tariffs and by devaluing their currencies,
but the way these measures affect a country's trade balance
is not what most of us think. Tariffs and currency intervention are ways of shifting resources from one set of economic
agents to another, and it is these shifts in resources that affect
the trade balance, mainly by affecting a country's savings and
investment rates.*

WHAT IS TRADE INTERVENTION, OR MORE specifically, what are the
policies and institutional constraints that affect exports, imports,
and the trade surplus? Most analysts will readily recognize that there are a
number of explicit interventionist policies aimed at affecting trade and the
trade balance. Import tariffs, as everyone knows, are an important form of
trade intervention. When a country places tariffs on its imports of foreign
goods and services, it tends to reduce foreign imports overall and so causes
that country's trade deficit to decline or its trade surplus to rise.

It may seem obvious why this would occur. Tariffs raise the cost of foreign
goods and services and so make them relatively less attractive for domestic
buyers. Because we usually buy less of what is more expensive, especially
when there are cheaper alternatives, we would assume that domestic buyers
would buy less of that good or service from abroad and more from domestic
producers, and so total imports would fall. This, most people believe, is why
tariffs affect a country's trade balance.

But the impact of tariffs on the trade surplus doesn't actually work like this. To see why, let us assume that a country that is running a trade deficit, which we will call Fredonia, imports a good—widgets—that it cannot make domestically and yet it must consume no matter what. Let us further assume that Fredonian households and businesses will consume a fixed amount of foreign widgets no matter what the price of the widget may be.

In this case would tariffs still affect Fredonia's trade balance? At first glance it seems that they shouldn't. If Fredonian consumers and businesses have to buy the same amount of widgets whether or not there are tariffs imposed on the import of widgets, and if they cannot produce widgets domestically, then imports won't fall, and so the trade balance will remain unchanged, right?

This is not an unlikely or impossible case by the way. We often hear, for example from various business lobbies based in Washington, that because the United States produces nothing that it imports from China, tariffs on Chinese goods or a forced appreciation of the renminbi will have no impact on the U.S. trade balance. If Americans cannot produce what China exports to the United States, the lobbyists say, trade intervention against China will merely raise the cost of consumption to American households without in any way affecting total U.S. production or the trade balance.

Aside from the fact that the United States does, or can, produce many of the things it imports from China, this argument is completely wrong, and it is wrong because of the misconception that tariffs affect the trade balance mainly or only by making imports less attractive relative to domestic production. This is not how tariffs work.

To see why we should return to the Fredonian case. In Fredonia a tariff on widgets will indeed cause a change in the Fredonian trade balance even if it has no impact on the total amount of widgets imported from abroad. Fredonia's trade deficit, in other words, will fall even as the amount of widgets it imports stays exactly the same because of the inelastic demand for widgets in a Fredonia that cannot make widgets itself.

To understand why this is the case, it is important to remember that the real impact of tariffs is the effect they have on real household income and domestic production, which then affect the relationship between total domestic savings and total domestic investment. As I pointed out in chapter 1, it is the gap between the two that defines the trade surplus or deficit.

The way a tariff works is actually fairly straightforward. A tariff raises the cost of foreign imports. Because real household income is a function of both the nominal amount of household income and the cost of goods and services that households purchase, raising the cost of a good, such as widgets, effectively reduces the real value of household income. For any given amount of income, after all, the higher the cost of the goods and services it consumes, the less real income the household has.

In this case, as real household income in Fredonia declines, total household consumption must decline with it. Why? Because as Fredonians must buy the same amount of widgets, given that they have to pay more for widgets, their purchases leave them with less money with which to consume other goods, and so their total consumption must decline. If you spend more on one good, you have less to spend on others.

If the Fredonian government does not use the additional tax revenues to increase government consumption, and if the total amount of the production in Fredonia is unchanged after the imposition of tariffs, then by definition the country's savings rate must rise. Savings, as we explained in chapter 1, are nothing more than the difference between total production and total consumption.

If Fredonia's total savings rise, as they must in this case, and if there is no change in domestic investment—say, for example, the only thing the Fredonian government did with the revenues generated by the tariff was to purchase U.S. government bonds—then Fredonia's trade deficit will automatically decline as its saving rates automatically rises. The tariff, in other words, reduced real Fredonian household income, and it was the reduction in Fredonian household income that caused the Fredonian trade deficit to decline, even though Fredonians imported as many widgets after the tariff as they ever did.

Notice that this has nothing to do with whether or not Fredonians suddenly become more or less lazy, thrifty, puritanical, or pleasure loving. Simply the imposition of the tariff itself automatically forced up the national savings rate by reducing household consumption, and this forced down the trade deficit.

This is really the key point about how tariffs affect the trade balance. If Fredonia is running a trade deficit, then it is true by definition that the total amount of investment in Fredonia must be greater than total savings in Fredonia. Why? Because if Fredonia is running a trade deficit, it must be importing capital to fund the trade deficit, and it would import capital only if the total amount of its domestic savings was insufficient to fund the total amount of its investment.[1]

Anything that changes the gap between Fredonia's investment and Fredonia's savings will affect Fredonia's trade deficit. If savings rise relative to investment, then by definition Fredonia's trade deficit must fall. If the tariffs caused Fredonian real household income to decline, and with it Fredonian household consumption, then Fredonia's savings rate by definition must have increased. Given no change in overall Fredonian production of goods and services, its total savings must have increased relative to its total investment. In that case its trade deficit must have declined.

Trade Intervention Affects the Savings Rate

This is an extremely simple and stylized example, of course, but the main point of the example is to suggest the mechanism by which tariffs affect a country's trade balance. It is not because foreign goods are relatively more expensive, and so Fredonians will buy fewer of them, that Fredonia's trade deficit will decline. It is because Fredonian consumption will decline in line with the decline in real household income. And notice that even though Fredonians bought exactly the same number of widgets, they had either to reduce their imports of some other good or increase their exports.

Roughly the same thing would have happened, by the way, if rather than imposing a tariff on widgets Fredonia had simply imposed a consumption tax on all goods consumed by households in Fredonia. In that case it is clear that foreign goods would be no more expensive than domestic goods in relative terms because all of them are taxed at the same rate.

But notice what happens to the gap between savings and investment. Just as in the case of tariffs, the consumption tax reduces real household income because households are able to buy fewer goods and services after the consumption tax is imposed. This causes a reduction in the total amount of their consumption. If total production of goods and services is unchanged, a consumption tax that causes Fredonians to reduce their domestic consumption will automatically increase their domestic savings rate, in exactly the same way that a tariff would.

Of course it is not at all clear that a consumption tax or a tariff would leave the total domestic production of goods and services unchanged. This would depend crucially on how the proceeds of that tax are spent. Depending on how this happens, the total production of goods and services can rise, decline, or remain unchanged.

We will discuss this more later in this book, but it is important to remember the main points of this exercise: the impact of a tariff on Fredonia's trade deficit, just like the impact of a consumption tax, is fully explained by the impact it has on the gap between Fredonian investment and Fredonian savings. By reducing domestic consumption, it forces up domestic savings. Because in our example there was no change in domestic investment, the excess of investment over savings narrowed, and with it, Fredonia's trade deficit narrowed.

Anything that reduces consumption, in other words, without changing total production or total investment, must cause an increase in exports relative to imports.[2] And notice that Fredonian savings went up without anyone exhorting the Fredonians to behave in a thriftier manner. Tariffs and consumption taxes always raise the savings rate and increase net exports by reducing the real value of disposable household income and so, presumably, by reducing household consumption.

Notice also that the net impact of tariffs and consumption taxes is broadly the same whether or not Fredonians can produce widgets or must import them all. The impact of the tariff works itself generally through the economy by shifting the gap between savings and investment, and it is not necessary, or even likely, that this shift will occur in the form of a change in widget imports. This is an extremely important point, which too many analysts misunderstand, and unfortunately their inability to understand leads to very serious policy mistakes.

In Europe, for example, one very common argument against Greece's leaving the euro and devaluing in order to regain competitiveness is that Greece cannot produce any of the things it imports. In that case, the analysts claim, devaluation will have no impact on Greece's massive trade deficit.

Whatever one thinks of the value of Greece's abandoning the euro (and however dubious and even absurd the claim that Greece cannot produce anything it imports), this cannot be a serious argument against leaving the euro. A devaluation will most certainly cause a shift in Greek consumption levels by changing the real value of household income. Depending on how the devaluation takes place and what other steps the Greek government takes, the impact on the trade deficit will be positive and fairly predictable— even if it is true that Greece cannot produce anything it imports. In that case it will either import less and spend more money domestically, or it will export more of some other good. There is no other possibility.

But what about Greek households—won't they be worse off if devaluation reduces the real value of household income? In some cases perhaps they will, but in this case probably not. Some employed households with secure jobs will be worse off, of course, because they will be able to buy less with their income, but because the country suffers from high levels of unemployment, those losses are likely to be more than offset by employment gains. As Greeks spend more of their money at home, this should cause domestic employment to rise. The additional income caused by an increase in unemployment will be greater the reduction in real income caused by the devaluation.

The fly in the Greek ointment is debt. Because devaluation can cause the level of debt—mostly denominated in euros—to soar, it may bring with it severe financial distress and corporate bankruptcies that more than offset the impact of devaluation. The positive employment impact of a Greek devaluation, in other words, can be more than offset by the negative employment impact of a financial distress.

But ignoring external debt, if a devaluation has a net positive employment effect—as it tends to in countries with high unemployment and stagnant growth—the overall income gains to households can easily exceed the losses, and so consumption will actually rise, but by less than total production of goods and services. This is especially the case if, as is the case in Greece, many unemployed workers receive workers' compensation. In that case Greek consumption will rise, but Greek savings will rise faster, and the trade deficit will almost certainly contract.

Currency Manipulation

Much of this is true in the same way when a country intervenes in its currency to reduce its value in terms of foreign exchange. Let us assume that rather than raise tariffs or consumption taxes the Fredonian central bank decided to reduce the value of the Fredonian franc by 20 percent.

How would it do so? The central bank would simply offer to purchase or sell unlimited amounts of Fredonian francs at a price equal to 20 percent below its current level. This is how any central bank that sets the exchange rate of its currency does so. In that case no one would buy Fredonian francs from anyone except the central bank, and so because all transactions must take place at this lower level, the value of the currency would automatically drop by 20 percent.

Is this a form of trade intervention? Clearly it is. Devaluing the Fredonian franc by 20 percent is the equivalent of putting in place a 25 percent tariff on all imported goods and offering a 20 percent subsidy to all Fredonian exports.

How does it work? Assume at first that there are ten Fredonian francs to the U.S. dollar. One Fredonian franc is worth, in other words, ten American cents. Further assume that it costs one U.S. dollar to make a widget in the United States and ten Fredonian francs to make one in Fredonia. The widgets have exactly the same price in the international markets.

If Fredonia devalues the Fredonian franc by 20 percent, the price of a Fredonian franc will become eight American cents. The ten Fredonian francs it cost to make a widget is now the equivalent of eighty American cents, so the Fredonian widget dropped in price by 20 percent in the international markets. American widgets, on the other hand, that cost one U.S. dollar to produce, are now worth 12.5 Fredonian francs, so the price of American widgets has increased in Fredonia by 25 percent.

So thanks to the devaluation it now costs 25 percent more for Fredonians to buy foreign goods, and Fredonian exporters can lower their prices in international markets by 20 percent without affecting their profit margins. This will allow them to expand sales dramatically. The combination of the two would cause a sharp contraction in Fredonia's trade deficit, but again, it is important to understand how this contraction occurs. It is not because higher import prices and lower export prices reduce imports and increase exports directly. It is because the devaluation of the Fredonian franc changes the savings and investment balance in Fredonia.

How so? As the Fredonian franc depreciates, the cost of all imports rises commensurately, and so as we showed earlier the real value of household income declines because any given amount of income is able to buy fewer things. As household income declines, household consumption is likely to decline too. This is because given that all imported goods cost more, Fredonian households have less money left over with which to buy domestic goods, and so they must reduce their total purchase of foreign and domestic goods in order to maintain their desired balance between household savings and household consumption.

Meanwhile what happens to total Fredonian production of goods and services? It rises, as capacity is increased to satisfy greater foreign demand for cheaper Fredonian goods. The Fredonian devaluation, in other words, has caused a reduction in total consumption and an increase in total production. This means that the Fredonian savings rate—the difference between the two—must have risen.

If it did indeed rise, perhaps even sharply, then unless there was an equivalent surge in Fredonia's investment rate (and it would have increased somewhat in order to increase capacity), the gap between total domestic savings and total domestic investment would have narrowed sharply. With it Fredonia's trade deficit would also have narrowed sharply.

Once again it is important to understand why currency intervention affects the trade balance. It does so by reducing Fredonian consumption and increasing Fredonian production, with the net impact, the increase in the savings rate, exceeding the impact of any increase in domestic investment. As savings rise relative to investment, the Fredonian trade deficit must narrow (or its surplus expand, if it was already running a surplus).

Exporting Capital Means Importing Demand

There is another way to think about the impact of a currency devaluation, although ultimately it is the same thing. Devaluing the currency is the equivalent of transferring resources from net importers (which includes primarily the household sector) to net exporters, which is composed mainly of the tradable goods sector.

In so doing it reduces consumption by reducing disposable household income and increases production by lowering input costs, thus pushing up the savings rate. But notice again that Fredonia's higher savings rate has nothing to do with Fredonians deciding to become thriftier or harder working. It was simply the automatic consequence of the devaluation.

In principle the household sector should be adamantly opposed to devaluing the currency because it reduces the real value of its household income, but as I suggested in the Greek example, there is a silver lining for them. If unemployment levels are high, or if the threat of a lot of new entrants into the labor market threatens to force down wages, the surge in production in the tradable goods sector will reduce unemployment or the threat of unemployment.

As more workers are hired, real household income will actually rise in the aggregate, as the lower real income from employed workers is more than compensated for by rising wages and the additional jobs for unemployed workers. This will cause overall household income to rise and with it overall household consumption.

But couldn't this rise in household consumption in fact cause total savings to decline? No, because as long as companies earn some profits and as long as households save at least some small portion of their income, then by definition household consumption cannot possibly rise faster than total production, and so total saving must rise.

In fact the impact on unemployment is why countries intervene in trade. Trade intervention may reduce the real value of existing household income, but it can cause employment to rise by more than the loss to households, and so in the aggregate households are better off. When economists say that a lower dollar will hurt American households by raising consumption costs, they are only partly right.

It will hurt employed American households as consumers, but it will help all American households as workers, and unless unemployment is extremely low, the latter impact should easily overwhelm the former and overall savings should rise (or debt decline). The purpose of trade intervention, in other words, is to increase domestic employment by appropriating foreign demand, and in doing so it automatically raises the national savings rate—whether or not there has been any change in the cultural propensity to save.

Notice something else in this case. By offering to sell Fredonian francs at 20 percent below their "natural" rate, the Fredonian central bank will be selling a lot of Fredonian francs and buying a lot of U.S. dollars. What does it do with these U.S. dollars? Obviously it must invest them abroad, probably in the United States as it buys U.S. Treasury bonds. This will cause Fredonian central bank reserves to grow—and this is simply another way of saying Fredonian capital exports will rise.

We have already said that net capital exports are the obverse of the current account surplus, and this process shows one of the automatic mechanisms by which this occurs. Fredonian intervention in the currency forces the Fredonian central bank to accumulate dollars, which it must export abroad. If on balance the Fredonian central bank's total capital exports exceed the net capital imports of the rest of the economy (because Fredonia had a trade deficit before it intervened in the currency, it had to have been a net capital importer), Fredonia's trade deficit will become a trade surplus. The amount of the trade surplus will be exactly equal to the excess of central bank capital exports over net non-central-bank capital imports.

This is an accounting identity that must hold. If we assume for the sake of simplicity that the net capital account ignoring the central bank is zero (i.e., non-central-bank Fredonians import as much capital as they export), then Fredonia's trade surplus will be exactly equal to the increase in Fredonia's central bank reserves. If Fredonia's central bank buys $50 billion a year to hold the Fredonian franc down, Fredonia's trade surplus will be exactly equal to $50 billion (remember that we are assuming for the sake of simplicity that the net nontrade part of the current account is effectively zero).

A lot of confusion persists about this important point. For example, we often hear commentators argue that if the People's Bank of China were to allow the value of the renminbi to rise, it would have no impact on the trade surplus because China is able to produce manufactured goods so cheaply. China would still be the low-cost seller and the rest of world would buy as much as ever from China and sell as little as ever to China. China's trade surplus, in other words, would not change.

This is almost total nonsense. The only possible way it could be true is if the amount of intervention in the renminbi was unaffected by the price level, and this is certainly not the case. If it were, the People's Bank of China should anyway immediately raise the value of the renminbi substantially in order to improve its terms of trade at no cost to employment.

But if a more expensive renminbi reduced the exporters' demand for renminbi, or increased importers' willingness to sell renminbi, then the total amount of central bank intervention would be less as the value of the renminbi rises. In this case, the People's Bank of China would be accumulating fewer U.S. dollars and so exporting less capital abroad.

By definition the less capital China exports abroad, the lower its trade surplus, so one way or the other an increase in the value of the renminbi must reduce the Chinese trade surplus as long as the higher value of the renminbi reduces the net amount of central bank intervention. The fact that it is sometimes hard to figure out the mechanism by which this reduction in the trade surplus might take place is irrelevant. It will nonetheless take place. If China exports less capital, its trade surplus will decline. This is an arithmetical necessity.

What happens if the market knows that the People's Bank of China is raising the value of the renminbi, and this induces capital inflow by private investors seeking to benefit from the rising renminbi? In fact nothing much happens.

The increase in inflows will increase the demand for renminbi, so it will increase central bank intervention by exactly the same amount. If you look only at the central bank's figures, its capital exports will actually rise, and this will seem to imply an increase in the trade surplus, but remember that the increase in capital exports by the People's Bank of China will be matched by an increase in private-sector capital inflows, so that net there is still a reduction in total Chinese capital exports. The trade surplus must decline.

What Happens If China Revalues the Renminbi?

It may help to understand how currency intervention works by examining what would happen to China if the central bank were to revalue the renminbi by some amount. Many people in China and abroad have argued that Beijing cannot afford to raise the value of the renminbi against the dollar because it would mean that China will take huge losses on its massive foreign exchange reserves. After all, if the renminbi rises by 10 percent against the dollar, with China holding over $3 trillion in reserves, the value of reserves will have necessarily declined by more than $300 billion in renminbi terms. So, the argument goes, raising the value of the renminbi will represent a loss of wealth for China.

This is almost completely wrong. China will not take losses anywhere close to that amount and may probably even take a gain if it revalues the currency. The mistake has to do with misunderstanding the impact of a currency change on the various relevant balance sheets.

Unfortunately this kind of confused thinking is nonetheless the source of some very strange claims. One English economist, for example, argued indignantly in 2009 that the United States was pressuring China to revalue the renminbi not because of trade rebalancing but rather because of a secret American scheme to reduce the amount that the U.S. government has to pay China on its People's Bank of China holdings of U.S. government bonds.[3]

Appreciation of the renminbi, according to this theory, represents a transfer of wealth from China to the United States because it effectively reduces the value of China's hoard of U.S. Treasury bonds. If China loses money, the theory continues, then someone must have made an equivalent profit, and the most likely culprit is the U.S. government, so, assuming China's reserves stand at $3 trillion, a 10 percent revaluation of the renminbi would represent a $300 billion transfer from China to the United States.

The claim, popular especially with conspiracy theorists, is confused to the point of nonsense and even violates simple arithmetic—after all, $100 owed by the U.S. government is worth exactly $100 whether or not China or anyone else changes the intervention levels of its currency. It is nonetheless an interesting argument because it shows just how poorly central bank reserves and their role in the trade balance are understood and how absurd are some of the claims made by "experts" about the global balance of payments. As such, this claim creates a useful point from which to explain the functioning of central bank reserves.

First of all, will China as an economic entity lose if the renminbi is revalued by, say, 10 percent? Leaving aside the vigorous discussion about whether or not a renminbi revaluation will increase China's long-term growth prospects (I think it will), the balance sheet impact of a revaluation depends on whether China is net long or net short dollars. Because a revaluation is largely a balance sheet affair, this is the only relevant question in deciding on what the immediate profit or loss a revaluation of the renminbi might produce.

There is no precise way of answering this question, because every single economic entity in China implicitly has some complex exposure to the dollar (by which I mean foreign currencies generally) through current and future transactions. Generally speaking, however, China is likely to gain from a revaluation because after the revaluation it will be exchanging the stuff it makes for stuff it buys from abroad at a better ratio.

The value of what it sells abroad, in other words, will rise relative to the value of what it buys from abroad, and if we could correctly capitalize those values on the balance sheet, it would probably show that the Chinese balance sheet would improve with a revaluation of the renminbi. Some economists might make a more sophisticated argument that because China is a net creditor—that is, it is net long dollars—it will lose by a revaluation of the renminbi. This argument also turns out to be wrong, but for more complex reasons, and to explain why we need to consider the difference between a real loss and a realized loss.

If you believe that the renminbi is undervalued, then you must accept that China takes a "real" loss every single time it exchanges a locally produced good or asset for a foreign one. After all, it is selling something at below its true value in exchange for something at above its true value. It does not "realize" the loss, however, until it revalues the renminbi to its "correct" value. In other words, the People's Bank of China, as the representative of China's net creditor status, will immediately realize a loss when the renminbi revalues.

But this loss did not occur because of the revaluation. It occurred the very day the trade took place. When a Chinese producer sold goods to the United States and took payment in U.S. dollars, there was an unrealized economic loss equal to the undervaluation of the renminbi. This unrealized loss was passed onto the People's Bank of China when it bought the dollars from the exporter and paid renminbi. This loss, however, will not actually show up until the renminbi is revalued, which forces the real loss to be realized (i.e., recognized as an accounting matter).

Postponing the revaluation, then, is not the way to avoid the loss—it is too late for that. The only way to avoid future additional loss is to stop making the exchange, which means, ironically, that the longer the People's Bank of China postpones the revaluation of the renminbi, the greater the real loss it will take because the more overvalued dollars it will have accumulated.

So a revaluation of the renminbi will not cause any real loss to China today. The loss already occurred but hasn't been realized. But if the renminbi is revalued by 10 percent, the value of the People's Bank of China's assets will immediately decline by around $300 billion in renminbi terms.[4] Because the Chinese measure their wealth in renminbi, isn't this a real additional loss for China?

No it is not. The only things China or any other country can do with foreign exchange reserves are pay for foreign imports or repay foreign obligations. Foreign reserves by definition cannot be spent at home, and so the real value of foreign reserves is the value of things a country can do with the reserves abroad. Of course if the value of the reserves drops 10 percent in renminbi terms when the People's Bank of China revalues the renminbi, so does the value of all those foreign payments—by definition they must go down by exactly the same amount in renminbi terms.

This means that China as an economic entity takes no loss on the dollars it had in its foreign currency reserves. It can buy and pay for just as much "stuff" after the revaluation as it could before the revaluation—and of course the real value of money is what you can buy with it. So the real value of the reserves hasn't changed at all—just the accounting value in renminbi—but this simply recognizes losses that were already taken long ago when the trade was first made, and should be a largely irrelevant number.

Wealth Is Transferred within China

But that doesn't mean nothing at all happened. Although the Chinese overall balance sheet is probably a little better off with the revaluation, within China there is a whole set of winners and losers. Who is whom depends on the structure of *individual* balance sheets. Basically everyone who is net long dollars against the renminbi loses in an appreciation, and everyone who is net short dollars against the renminbi wins.

In practice this has important implications. Of course the People's Bank of China is a big loser. It has a hugely mismatched balance sheet in which it is long dollars against renminbi by around $3 trillion. Its balance sheet is mismatched because to fund the $3 trillion of dollar assets it has $3 trillion in renminbi liabilities (the People's Bank of China is actually probably insolvent).[5] As the dollar depreciates 10 percent against the renminbi, the value of the foreign exchange assets drops relative to renminbi by that amount, but of course the value of renminbi liabilities remains unchanged. The People's Bank of China, in other words, loses the renminbi equivalent of $300 billion of assets with no commensurate loss of liabilities, and so it takes a huge net loss.

There are other losers. Exporters and their employees, too, are naturally long dollars because of the nature of their business, and so they would lose from a revaluation. They are long dollars because more of the net value of their current and future production less current and future costs is denominated in dollars (they are "sticky" to dollar prices)—for example, labor costs, land, and almost all other inputs except imported components are valued in renminbi, whereas most revenues are valued in dollars.

But if China as a whole takes no loss on the revaluation, then for every loser in China there must be a winner. And who is it that wins? It turns out that nearly everyone else in China wins because everyone in the country is implicitly short dollars to the extent that there are imported goods in their life.

The local tea seller is short dollars if his tea is delivered to him in gas-guzzling trucks, as is the family planning to visit Bali next year, as is the local provider of French perfumes, as is a teenager who wants to buy Nike shoes, and so pay for the corporate sponsorship of a Brazilian soccer star playing for a Spanish team. Every household and nearly every business in China is, in one way or another, an importer (and this is true in every country), so unless they own a lot of assets abroad they are effectively short dollars and will benefit from an appreciation in the renminbi.

Revaluing the renminbi, in other words, is important and significant because it represents a shift of wealth, largely from the People's Bank of China, exporters, and wealthy Chinese residents who have stashed away a lot of their money in foreign banks, in favor of the rest of the country. Because much of this shift of wealth benefits households at the expense of the state and manufacturers, one of the automatic consequences of a revaluation will be an increase in household wealth and, with it, household consumption. Of course if household consumption rises, then total savings will decline.

This is why revaluation is an important part of China's rebalancing strategy—it shifts income from the low-consuming state to higher consuming households and so increases both household and national consumption. But there is more. As household consumption increases, the higher renminbi may reduce production in the tradable goods sector. The combination of higher consumption and lower production reduces the savings rate even more. If there is no change in investment, or if any reduction in investment is lower than the reduction in savings, China's trade surplus will automatically decline even further.

At the risk of excess repetition, it is worth pointing out again that the revaluation of the renminbi automatically shifted income within China and caused the savings rate to decline. For this to happen it was wholly unnecessary that the Chinese reduced their fabled cultural propensity to save, or that the population aged, or that a younger, post–Cultural Revolution generation infused households with their spendthrift ways. Savings in China would automatically decline simply because the renminbi was revalued, in exactly the same way (albeit in an opposite directions) that a devaluation by Fredonia caused the savings rate to rise.

We can generalize from this example to consider that many kinds of wealth transfers within the country can have an impact on the trade balance—and this is the secret to understanding how policies affect the savings rate. Just as the case of a revaluation of the renminbi implies a transfer of wealth from the People's Bank of China to Chinese households, and so is likely to increase consumption, other transfers from the state sector to households can have the same effect.

Does China Need a Social Safety Net?

Consider, for example, the issue of China's weak social safety net. Many analysts argue that one reason for the high Chinese savings rate (and so high trade surplus) is that Chinese households lack an adequate social safety net. As this 2010 *Washington Post* article puts it,

> The key reason Chinese save so much and consume so little, experts say, is because without dependable government payments, they need to sock

away money for the future—for medical emergencies, for children's educational expenses, as a guarantee against a job loss or to help elderly parents.

"When a person has no medical insurance, unemployment insurance or endowment insurance, how can that person dare spend all their money?" said Tang Jun, a sociology researcher with the China Academy of Social Sciences. "The Chinese people are a nationality that likes saving money. . . . . Ordinary people will only feel relieved about consuming if they don't have to worry about not having money when they get old and not having money to go to the hospital."[6]

According to this argument, because educational and medical costs are extremely high and there is little in the way of unemployment or retirement benefits for most Chinese, it is no surprise that Chinese households save an extraordinarily high proportion of their income for precautionary motives. The World Bank has even argued that one of the most important steps China can take in rebalancing is substantially improving the social safety net available to Chinese households.

There are two problems with this argument. First, although the national savings rate in China is extraordinarily high, the household savings rate is not. It is high, but well in line with those of many other Asian countries, and lower than some. High savings rates in China reflect fairly high savings at the household level and also high savings at the corporate and government levels. They are consequences of a variety of structural and policy conditions that have forced consumption down by reducing the household share of income. While it may seem plausible to argue that a lack of a social safety net explains why households save so much, it cannot possibly be an explanation for why corporations and governments save so much.

The second problem is that we see very high savings rates in a number of Asian countries that follow similar policies that, I argue (in this and the next chapter), automatically force up the national savings rate. These policies are all variations on the Japanese growth model, which included as components of its growth strategy an undervalued currency, lagging wage growth, and financial repression.

All these countries had high savings rates during the period in which they implemented these policies and conditions, but not all of them had weak social safety nets. On the contrary, Japan, Singapore, and South Korea, for example, all had relatively robust social safety nets, and yet they nonetheless also had high savings rates. In fact it is hard, looking at the world in general, to argue that countries with better social safety nets have lower savings rates than countries with worse social safety nets. This claim would certainly not fit observations of European and U.S. savings rates (Europe tends to have both a better social safety net and higher savings rates), nor would it explain why as Beijing has worked to improve the social safety net in China over the past five years, the savings rate has increased, and not declined.

So does China's weak social safety net matter, and won't improving it lower the Chinese savings rate? Yes, it matters, but not in the way most analysts think. China's weak social safety net has indeed had an impact on helping to create China's high savings rate, but the impact occurred not because of the need for precautionary savings as much as because it is the consequence of the erosion of Chinese household wealth.

Twenty or thirty years ago, most Chinese belonged to a work unit, which took care of their employment, their educational expenses, their medical needs, and their retirement. As part of China's liberalization, most of these benefits were lost. This loss represented, effectively, a transfer of wealth from households to the state since what was once a government liability became a household liability. It is this reduction in household wealth, relative to the country's overall production of goods and services, which forced up the savings rate. Chinese households, in other words, consumed less than they otherwise might have because their wealth decreased in relative terms thanks to the erosion of their social safety net, and this automatically forced up the savings rate.

This explanation has important implications for policy. It means, for example, that the popular claim, and one pushed forcefully by the World Bank, that Chinese consumption can be raised—that is, Chinese savings reduced—by putting into place a robust social safety net, is incomplete. The key is not the existence of a social safety net but rather the net impact of a social safety net on Chinese household wealth. This is a point made, by the way, by Justin Yifu Lin, chief economist for the World Bank, in a 2011 speech:

> In recent debates about the rebalancing toward domestic demand in China, much is made of the need for social safety nets to stimulate domestic demand. I will argue that the need for social safety net is for the purposes of social harmony rather than for increasing the ratio of consumption in China. This is because while households may increase the propensity for consumption with improved social safety nets, the government needs to increase savings in order to accumulate the provision funds for covering the costs of pension and other social spending. As a result, the total aggregate savings of private households and the government may not change much.[7]

If the social safety net is paid for by additional transfers from the household sector—for example in the form of higher taxes or, as we show in the next chapter, by government borrowing—it will have almost no net impact on household consumption or on national savings. In fact because a robust social safety net might not be credible for many years, so that Chinese households register their lower disposable income as they pay for the benefits but fail to include the value of those benefits in their calculation of wealth, a stronger social safety net may actually reduce consumption in the short term.

For it to be effective in reducing Chinese savings, the implementation of a social safety net has to be paid for not by Chinese households but rather by the state sector. The state must, in other words, liquidate assets to pay for the social safety net or else it will not have any impact on overall consumption.

This is borne out by observation. Many observers have been surprised by the fact that in the past few years the Chinese government has taken steps to improve the Chinese social safety net but consumption has continued to decline as a share of GDP and savings to rise. But they should not have been surprised. Improvements in the social safety net that are paid for by households will have a limited impact on their overall wealth, and so on their savings rate. An increase in the household consumption share of GDP will require a real transfer of wealth from the state sector to the household sector. We return to this concept later in this book.

CHAPTER THREE

The Many Forms of Trade Intervention

Obvious forms of trade intervention, like import tariffs and currency manipulation, affect a country's trade balance by affecting the savings and investment rates. It should be clear that this implies that a very wide variety of policies and institutional structures, intentionally or not, are forms of trade intervention if they include any explicit or hidden tax transfer that affects the relationship among total production, total consumption, and total investment.

A S THE DISCUSSION OF THE SOCIAL safety net in the previous chapter suggests, once we fully understand the mechanism by which obvious forms of trade intervention, like currency manipulation or import tariffs, actually affect the trade balance, it will become clear that there is a wide variety of policies and institutional structures that can have significant impacts on the trade balance, even when they may at first seem unrelated to trade. Anything that affects the gap between savings and investment, it turns out, must automatically affect the trade balance.

Of course this also means that because anything that affects the gap between production and consumption also affects the savings rate, it must also affect the gap between savings and investment. This is the key point. A very large number of policies or conditions are likely to affect production or consumption or the relationship between the two, in which case these policies or conditions are directly or indirectly also likely to affect the balance of trade. For this reason they are functionally equivalent to trade policies even if they are not intended as such.

The fact that at first glance they may seem to have nothing to do directly with trade is not at all relevant, but it certainly creates many confused claims in the debate over trade. One of the perhaps more intriguing factors that affect the trade balance, for example, is the process of large-scale environmental degradation. Trade unions in the United States often argue that weak environmental standards in Mexico, Vietnam, and other poor countries undermine the U.S. tradable goods sector because they act as a kind of subsidy to local manufacturers. In order to redress the implicit subsidy, the trade unions often ask for tariffs roughly equal to the cost that companies would have incurred if they had not been able to dispose so cavalierly of their waste products.

But while it may well be true that environmental degradation is a kind of subsidy, the analysis of its full impact on trade is incomplete until it explains how environmental degradation affects the overall gap between savings and investment. In fact it turns out that the impact on the trade balance is greater than simply the implicit subsidy. Environmental degradation, as we will see, can have a complex but very predictable impact on that gap.

To take one example of how this might happen, if domestic regulations or social conditions in Indonesia allow a local paint manufacturer to dump untreated chemicals into the river at the edge of the factory, these must certainly lower local paint manufacturing costs. Permitting the unconstrained dumping of chemicals and other toxic wastes, in that sense, clearly acts as a subsidy that allows the Indonesian paint manufacturer to expand capacity at the expense of foreign competitors, who might not be able to dispose of unwanted chemicals quite so cheaply and easily. It will make Indonesian products more competitive in the international markets than they might otherwise have been, and so spur higher levels of Indonesian production. Unless unemployment is close to zero, higher Indonesian paint production will not crowd out other Indonesian production, and so total Indonesian production of goods and services will rise, perhaps by as much as the increase in Indonesian production and exports of paint.

But this is not the end of the story. The unconstrained dumping of toxic waste also affects the overall level of Indonesian consumption. Why? Because countries with high levels of environmental degradation are likely to have rising health problems, and households know this from experience. Even if they don't know how the specific actions of the company will affect their health, over many years of declining health standards they will have learned to expect rising health care costs.

If members of an Indonesian household believe that in the future they are likely to have a significant and growing health liability, and that the family will incur higher expenses associated with that health liability, including possibly that members of the household might have to quit working for extended periods of time or retire earlier than otherwise, the real wealth of that household today is effectively reduced. Expected losses or expenses in the future are the same as a reduction in today's wealth.

As household wealth is reduced, so is household consumption. This is often called the wealth effect. People who feel poorer will reduce their consumption, and lower consumption today out of regular wages of course means an increase in the savings rate. This is just another way of saying that most households save in part to cover future medical costs, and as expected medical costs rise, households save more.

But notice that two different things are occurring. First, Indonesian producers are producing more paint because their lower environmental costs allow them to take market share from their foreign competitors. Second, Indonesian households are consuming less than they otherwise might have to save for future health problems.

The combination of higher Indonesian production and lower Indonesian consumption of course has a double impact on forcing up the Indonesian savings rate. A rise in savings must affect the gap between savings and investment. Of course investment may well rise too as Indonesian companies increase paint-making capacity, but as long as workers save part of their income and companies earn more than their debt servicing costs the total increase in investment must be smaller than the total increase in savings. The trade impact of a weak environmental regime, in other words, is not just the implicit subsidy to the tradable goods sector but also the reduced household consumption caused by future health concerns, both of which can push up the trade surplus. This is how environmental degradation can cause a country's trade surplus to rise even while making the country poorer.

Another factor that may at first seem unrelated to trade but in fact can have a significant trade impact is the state of local housing and stock markets. This was most evident recently in the United States and several peripheral European countries. These countries experienced soaring asset markets over the decade prior to the crisis, perhaps driven by rapidly expanding domestic liquidity.

How Changes in Wealth Affect Savings

When stock and real estate markets soar in value, owners of these assets can feel a surge in personal wealth. The perceived increase in wealth can be so great that households substantially increase consumption out of current income. In a sense they are counting on the higher value of their homes and investment portfolios to cover their retirement needs, or unexpected medical costs, and so save less out of current income for those purposes.

If stock and real estate ownership is widely distributed we can even experience the seeming paradox of households assuming that their savings are rising significantly even as the country's actual savings rate declines. As savings decline relative to GDP and investment (in fact investment may even rise to satisfy speculative demand for additional housing), the consequence must be that imports grow much faster than exports and the country's trade deficit will expand or its trade surplus contract.

We will come back to this when we discuss financial repression and the wealth effect at the end of this chapter, and we will see how changes in wealth affect a country's trade balance, but before doing so it might be worthwhile to consider the impact on savings of changes in a country's price level. Can unexpected inflation, to take the example that we tend most to worry about, affect a country's savings rate?

It most certainly can. Unexpected inflation tends to help borrowers and hurt lenders by reducing the real value of financial obligations. If this affects the country's savings and investment rates, which of course it must, it also must automatically have a trade impact, although exactly how depends on the structure of the economy.

In most cases the household sector is a net lender, saving a portion of its income in the form of bank deposits. The household sector also is a net lender if it expects future pension payments or other fixed income revenues for which it has already paid. Inflation, then, usually transfers wealth from households to net borrowers, which usually include the government and large corporations (if they borrowed to buy either real assets or operations whose products can be easily repriced with inflation), as well as other households that may have speculated on stocks, commodities, or real estate with borrowed money.

But because in the aggregate the household sector is usually a net lender, not a net borrower, as inflation rises, household wealth usually declines, and with it, household consumption declines too. If household consumption declines faster than growth in the economy, the savings rate must rise, although if inflation is associated with negative economic growth, as it usually is, for example, under conditions of very high inflation, the savings rate can rise even as overall savings decline (i.e., savings are a larger share of a smaller economic pie).

What if inflation rises so quickly that households despair about their ability to maintain the value of their savings? In that case rising inflation may actually cause what looks like an increase in consumption. Households may accelerate their purchase of consumer goods as a way of locking in lower current prices, in which case it actually looks like the rise in inflation has caused the savings rate to drop. In fact this isn't what happens, although as far as its impact on the trade balance, this might as well have happened. Why? Because the increased purchase of consumption goods does not really represent consumption. It is a form of investment, so that the increase in savings is matched by an equivalent increase in investment.

The impact of inflation on the trade balance, then, can be quite complex. It can raise the savings rate by undermining household wealth, which should cause an improvement in the trade balance, but if high and rising inflation causes households to switch their savings from bank deposits to consumer goods, it can cause an equivalent increase in investment that looks like a reduction in savings, so neutralizing the positive impact on the balance of trade. If inflation slows the economy and causes a rise in unemployment, it will further cause GDP to drop faster than consumption as workers lose their jobs, which then pushes down the savings rate and so worsens the trade balance.

The complex impact of inflation on savings is an important point to remember. Analysts often blithely suggest that Europe and China can deal with a portion of their respective banking problems simply by inflating the money supply. As collateral value or cash flow from operations grows more quickly than debt-servicing costs, this will presumably help banks reduce their nonperforming loans.

This may well be true, but it comes at the expense of net lenders to the banking system—depositors. For that reason by reducing real household wealth inflation also forces down real household consumption. For countries with excessively high consumption rates, like peripheral Europe, this might not be a bad thing unless done to excess, but for countries like Germany and China, for reasons that we discuss in chapters 4 and 6, forcing up the savings rate can only make a bad problem worse. Ironically the only "good" inflation in those countries—good in the sense that it forces down the savings rate—must come with rising unemployment. Otherwise it may actually increase savings, as we will see later in this chapter when we discuss financial repression.

Wage Growth

There are a number of non-trade-related domestic factors we have discussed, like weak environmental regulations, soaring asset markets, or unexpected inflation, that affect a country's trade balance by altering the gap between savings and investment, but there are three domestic policies or institutional conditions that are especially important—and especially relevant in discussing the trade surpluses in East Asia. Many Asian countries have followed the growth model established in the 1960s and 1970s by Japan, and this growth model includes crucially these three conditions:

1. Systematically undervalued currencies, in which the central bank intervenes in the currency to reduce its exchange value
2. Relatively low wage growth, in which wages grow more slowly than improvements in worker productivity
3. Financial repression, in which the state allocates credit and the central bank forces interest rates to below their natural or equilibrium rate

We have already discussed the first of these three in chapter 2. To recap, an undervalued currency, by raising the costs of imports, acts as a kind of consumption tax for households and so reduces disposable household income. With lower disposable household income usually comes lower household consumption. But taxes are just transfers of resources from one group to another. In this and similar cases the proceeds of this hidden "undervaluation" tax are effectively transferred to manufacturers of tradable goods, and so are used to subsidize production in the tradable goods sector, which consequently is likely to rise.

As we showed in chapter 2, the combination of lower consumption and higher production automatically causes a surge in the savings rate. Investment is also likely to rise somewhat in the tradable goods sector, given the expected rise in profitability of that sector, but of course not nearly as much as the increase in savings. This is why undervalued currencies typically tend to create trade surpluses for countries that intervene to lower the value of their currencies.

More or less the same process occurs in what may seem at first like a radically different condition—that of lagging wage growth relative to the growth in the average worker's productivity. When wages grow more slowly than productivity, there is a tax transfer from one group of actors to another in the economy, and just like the implicit tax transfer associated with an undervalued currency, this transfer tends to push up the savings rate and so causes an increase in exports relative to imports.

It is important to understand just how this occurs because in many developing countries, and even in many rich ones like Germany in the past decade, the average worker's wage has grown, but not as quickly as the average worker's productivity. The gap between the two has an automatic impact both on the national savings rate and on the country's trade surplus.

Why? Because in a state of equilibrium, and over long periods of time, the growth in workers' average wage should match the growth in their average productivity. As this happens, average workers' share of what they produce stays constant and, because their consumption is likely to be determined by their earnings, which are a constant share of total production, they are also likely to consume a more or less constant share of what they produce.

Countries can go for long periods of time violating this equilibrium condition, but when wages rise faster than productivity for many years, or when they rise more slowly, there is effectively a transfer of the share of ownership of the country's economy—in the former case workers get a rising share and in the latter they get a declining share. In fact we often see in developing countries long periods in which wage growth lags productivity growth. There are several reasons this can happen. For example in many of the Asian countries during the second half of the twentieth century, while in the early stages of their development economic growth was accompanied by large-scale migration from the poor countryside to the urban and industrial centers in which jobs were being created.

If rural migration was sufficiently large, it tended to repress wage growth. This made it fairly common for worker productivity to grow quickly as less productive rural workers and peasants moved to the industrial centers, where their productivity was much higher, but for wages to fail to keep pace. When this happens wage growth will lag productivity growth and the worker's share of total income will decline, even as total income might rise.

There can also be legal and institutional impediments to rising worker wages. For example in countries where unions are prohibited, or where they work primarily in the interest of bosses and the government, workers may not have the political power to force wages up, and employers can take steps to increase their profitability at the expense of workers. In addition in some countries, like China with its complex *hukou* system, workers may have limited legal residence rights when they move away from their original areas of residence. This keeps them at the mercy of unscrupulous employers and their de facto allies, the police and legal system.

Whatever the reason, the difference in growth rate between wages and productivity can automatically affect the country's saving rate and therefore its balance of trade. How so? Because if workers are forced to retain a declining share of what they produce—which is all that is meant when productivity growth outstrips wage growth—the gap between the total production of goods and services and total household income is likely to grow. Because household consumption is largely a function of household income and household wealth, the growing gap between the total goods and services produced in a country and that country's total consumption will normally result in an automatic rise in the national savings rate.

This isn't always necessarily the case. In the United States the gap between the growth in workers' wages and workers' productivity during the past decade did not lead to a declining share of consumption mainly because, thanks to a booming real estate and stock market, where much household wealth is concentrated, households perceived their overall wealth to have grown faster than productivity.

American households were able to turn to borrowing to increase their consumption, and their overall savings rate actually declined, but this is because the increase in household wealth more than compensated for the reduction in the worker's share of income. When, as is more normally the case, there isn't a counterbalance to the declining share of workers' wages, consumption is likely to decline as a share of total production and, with it, the savings rate to rise. And as long as the consequential increase in investment is less than the increase in savings, exports must grow relative to imports.

Trade Policy as the Implicit Consequence of Transfers

Notice how similar this is to the impact of an undervalued currency. In the latter case there is a hidden tax on households that serves to reduce disposable household income and, with it, household consumption. The same occurs in the former case. The growing gap between wages and productivity is just another hidden tax that transfers wealth from workers to employers. In both cases the tax effectively represents a transfer of resources from households, and resources available for household consumption, to a producing sector of the economy.

And in both cases the transfer of resources is a kind of subsidy that spurs growth in the production of goods and services while repressing household consumption growth. The net result is that there is upward pressure on the production of goods and services and downward pressure on consumption. Because, once again, savings are the difference between total production and total consumption, the savings rate is forced up, and even though the subsidy to producers may cause an increase in total investment, if it is less than the increase in savings the trade surplus must rise.

We can generalize from these examples. Any policies that lead to transfers of resources from one sector of the economy to another are effectively explicit or hidden taxes and explicit or hidden subsidies. To the extent that these taxes affect total production or total consumption, and they often if not nearly always do, they implicitly have an impact on the balance of trade.

The trade impact, we should remember, may not have been an original intention of the policy, but it is an automatic outcome. For example, as we saw in chapter 2 the erosion of China's social safety net in the past two decades was clearly not intended as a trade policy, but it has had a trade impact because it shifts resources from households to businesses. These policies nearly always work the same way. Typically in order to spur employment growth policymakers put into place policies that effectively subsidize certain classes of employers. All subsidies must be paid for, of course, and it is usually, although not always, the household sector that pays.

In case it is not the household sector that pays, the trade impact can be minor or hard to predict. For example, let us assume that South Korea decides to subsidize steelmakers by providing them with low-cost energy. It pays for these subsidies by raising corporate taxes or by forcing the local energy providers to take losses. In that case the subsidy to the steel producers is paid for by other businesses and the result is a transfer of resources from one set of businesses to steel producers.

The trade impact of such a subsidy is hard to measure without a lot more information and in fact may be minimal. If Korean steel producers are much less productive than businesses in general, or than the energy sector, and if there is no net impact on employment and wages, the net result might even be an increase in Korean imports relative to exports. This is because the amount of additional steel production is less than the amount of fore-gone domestic production of other goods and services, and so with total production declining relative to total consumption, the national savings rate automatically declines.

Far more common, however, is for the implicit subsidies to be paid for directly or indirectly by the household sector, in which case the trade impact can be pretty easy to determine. If households pay for subsidies provided to producers, whether they pay through explicit taxes—like in Brazil during its growth miracle in the 1960s and early 1970s, during which time high income taxes paid for most production and infrastructure subsidies—or in the form of hidden taxes, like the ones we are discussing in this chapter and the previous one, then household consumption growth is likely to lag the growth in total output and the savings rate must automatically rise.

To take another example, again from China, an important part of the industrialization process, and one open to serious abuse, is the ability of local policymakers to acquire agricultural land from local farmers, and then switch the zoning to more valuable commercial use. In 2010 in the town of Wukan, in Guangdong province, abuses were so widespread that in December the villagers threw out party officials and eventually won the right to elect their own. According to a *Financial Times* article published two months later in 2012,

> An essay in the state-owned People's Daily said abuse of power over land acquisition was "damaging people's rights." Some grassroots cad-res, it said, had "lost their sense of purpose." Wen Jiabao, the premier whose progressive-sounding interjections rarely gel with actual policy, opined: "We can no longer sacrifice farmers' land rights to lower the cost of industrialisation."[1]

The sacrificing of farmers' land rights to lower the cost of industrialization is not just potentially damaging to political rights, it also can have a trade impact. The land transfers represent a transfer of wealth, often substantial, from farmers to the state, industrial companies, real estate developers, and the very wealthy.

Once again, as in other cases we have looked at, it has the effect of reducing household income (or, more properly, household wealth) while boosting GDP by reducing the costs of acquiring land for business and investment. The net impact, of course, is that farmers whose wealth has been thus expropriated, or who worry that it might happen to them, reduce their consumption and increase their savings even as GDP growth is goosed. As an automatic consequence the Chinese savings rate rises faster than investment (because even if investment is increased the full value of the transfer is not converted into investment) and with it the trade surplus must rise too.

As significant as these various indirect transfers are, there may be one that is far more significant than any of them. Earlier in this chapter I claimed that there were three domestic policies or institutional conditions that were especially important in affecting the trade balance of the various countries that followed what is sometimes called the Japanese development model or the Asian model. The first two are systematically undervalued currencies and lagging wage growth relative to productivity growth. The third important factor, I argued, is financial repression.

Financial Repression

Financial repression is not always well understood, but in fact it can often be, and usually is, the most powerful of all the policies or conditions that generate trade imbalances and is at the heart of Chinese and Asian overall imbalances. Financial repression matters to trade even more than undervalued currencies, although, unfortunately, it rarely enters into the debate on trade imbalances.

What is a financially repressed system, and why does it matter? In a recent article Carmen M. Reinhart, Jacob F. Kierkegaard, and M. Belen Sbrancia described a financially repressed system this way:

> Financial repression occurs when governments implement policies to channel to themselves funds that in a deregulated market environment would go elsewhere. Policies include directed lending to the government by captive domestic audiences (such as pension funds or domestic banks), explicit or implicit caps on interest rates, regulation of cross-border capital movements, and (generally) a tighter connection between government and banks, either explicitly through public ownership of some of the banks or through heavy "moral suasion."
>
> Financial repression is also sometimes associated with relatively high reserve requirements (or liquidity requirements), securities transaction taxes, prohibition of gold purchases, or the placement of significant amounts of government debt that is nonmarketable. In the current policy discussion, financial repression issues come under the broad umbrella of "macroprudential regulation," which refers to government efforts to ensure the health of an entire financial system.[2]

As the passage implies, most savings in financial repressed countries, like most of the countries that followed the Asian development model, are in the form of bank deposits. The banks, furthermore, are controlled by the monetary authorities that determine the direction of credit, socialize the risks, and set interest rates. Financial repression is a way of describing a system in which the rates of return and the direction of investment of domestic savings are not determined by market conditions and individual preferences but rather are heavily controlled and directed by financial or political authorities. At the extreme the financial system is often little more than the fiscal agent of the government.

The key point for this discussion on trade is that if the central bank—or whichever institution has the appropriate responsibility—sets at an excessively high level the rates that household savers earn on their savings, it is effectively transferring resources from borrowers to depositors. If it sets the rate excessively low, of course, it does exactly the opposite.

In most countries that create the conditions of financial repression—for example, the countries that broadly followed the Asian or Japanese development model—interest rates have been set extremely low. Normally under these circumstances we would expect the losers in the system, the depositors, to opt out of depositing their savings in local banks, but it is extremely difficult for them to do so. There are usually significant restrictions on their ability to take capital out of the country, and there are few local investment alternatives that provide similar levels of safety and liquidity.

Depositors, in other words, have no choice but to accept very low deposit rates on their savings, which are then transferred through the banking system to borrowers, who benefit from these very low rates. Very low lending and deposit rates create a powerful mechanism for using household savings to boost growth by heavily subsidizing the cost of capital.

The ones who lose under conditions of financial repression are net depositors, who tend for the most part to be the household sector. The ones who win are net borrowers, and in most countries in which financial repression is a significant policy tool, these tend to be local and central governments, infrastructure investors, corporations and manufacturers, and real estate developers. Financial repression transfers wealth from the former to the latter.

Notice yet again how similar this policy is to currency undervaluation or lagging wage growth in its impact on trade. Just as in the previous two cases, under conditions of financial repression there is effectively a hidden tax on households that serves to reduce disposable household income and, with it, household consumption.

Also, as in the previous cases, the tax represented a transfer of resources from households—resources otherwise available for household consumption—to the sector of the economy that generates production and economic activity. In the two previous cases these sectors were the tradable goods sector and employers generally. In the case of financial repression the transfers effectively subsidize borrowers.

If most borrowing is limited to the state sector, large corporations, infrastructure investors, real estate developers, and others that contribute to economic activity, the transfer of resources is once again a kind of subsidy that spurs growth in the production of goods and services while repressing household consumption growth. The net result once again is that there is upward pressure on the production of goods and services and downward pressure on consumption. And once again, as we saw in other consumption-repressing policies, the savings rate is automatically forced up, and even though the subsidy to producers may cause an increase in total investment, it is less than the increase in savings, and so the trade surplus must rise.

Higher Interest Rates and Household Wealth

The negative impact of financial repression on consumption may at first seem surprising, or even counterintuitive. We are used to thinking that there is a positive correlation between interest rates and the savings rate. When interest rates decline, in other words, savings are expected to decline too.

But this is not necessarily the case. How do interest rates normally affect the savings and consumption rate? The mainstream view, of course, is that there should be a negative correlation between interest rates and consumption. In other words, when interest rates rise, households should save more and so consume less out of current income.

Why? One reason may be that savings are simply postponed consumption, and we are willing to postpone consumption if we are paid enough to do so. The more you pay me to save in the form of a high interest rate, in other words, the more I save out of current income, and so the less I consume today in order that I can consume even more tomorrow. The same thing happens, by the way, when rising interest rates cause the cost of consumer financing to rise, and so discourage the use of credit cards for consumption today.

But there is another reason why interest rates may be positively correlated with savings. Typically we associate rising interest rates with declining stock, real estate, and bond prices. If most of our wealth consists of these three kinds of assets, then higher interest rates should be associated with a decline in our wealth, and because we feel poorer, we reduce our consumption rate.

This seems fairly plausible too. When we feel richer we consume more out of current income.

In both of these cases rising interest rates are assumed to bring declining consumption and higher savings. This relationship seems to be supported by the data in many countries.

But the first explanation—that as you increase the reward for postponing consumption, households save more—is not wholly convincing. It is hard to believe that people really think this way about savings, and if they did, it would seem that unless there were an enormous preference for liquidity, in any country in which deposit rates were negative in real terms (i.e., the deposit rate were lower than inflation, so that households were effectively paying, not getting paid, to postpone consumption) consumption rates would rise to 100 percent or more.

This certainly isn't the case. In China, for example, deposit rates are seriously negative and have been negative for many years, and yet the household savings rate is nonetheless very high. In fact it seems that, as a rule, countries with repressed interest rates have higher, not lower savings rates.

What's more, there are ample U.S. historical data that suggest that when interest rate declines have coincided with falling, not rising, stock and real estate markets, the savings rate usually rises rather than declines. This certainly seems to have been the case in the United States and Europe since the onset of the crisis—declining interest rates coupled with declining real estate and asset prices have led to higher, not lower, household savings rates. It suggests, in other words, that in deciding how much they will consume households seem to care mainly about their wealth, not about the reward for postponing consumption.

If it is the wealth effect, and not the consumption-postponement effect, that really drives changes in savings and consumption rates, then raising rates would reduce consumption only if there was a negative correlation between interest rates and wealth. There clearly is in the United States, where most household wealth consists of real estate and stock and bonds portfolios.

But is there a negative correlation between the two in a financially repressed country like China? Probably not. Most Chinese savings, at least until recently, have been in the form of bank deposits. In a financial system in which deposit rates are set by the central bank, the value of bank deposits is positively, not negatively, correlated with the deposit rate. Chinese households, in other words, should feel richer when the deposit rate rises and poorer when it declines, in which case rising rates should be associated with rising, not declining, consumption.

This is a very important point and one barely understood by most commentators on China and perhaps even in the People's Bank of China. If deposit rates do not reflect market conditions—most important, inflation rates—but are simply set by the central bank in order to achieve policy objectives, then bank depositors, who measure their wealth in terms of the expected real return on their deposits, should welcome rising rates and deplore declining rates. The former should make them feel richer and so increase their consumption and the latter make them feel poorer.

One way in which this happens was explained to me in class by one of my Peking University undergraduates shortly after the People's Bank of China had reduced deposit rates a few years ago. According to my student, her aunt was planning to save a fixed amount of money for when her twelve-year-old son turned eighteen and was slated to go to university. She had a certain amount of money already saved, but not enough, so she needed to add to her savings every month to achieve her target.

How did she calculate the amount she needed to add to her savings? The process was fairly straightforward. She knew that she needed to add a fixed amount of savings every month so that, over six years, her total savings would have matched her target.

Every month she received interest on her existing deposit, so she took out of her monthly paycheck whatever the additional amount she needed to meet her monthly target. When the People's Bank of China reduced deposit rates, of course, she had to withdraw a larger amount from her monthly paycheck to make up the difference. This left her with less money out of her monthly paycheck for other expenditures. Lower deposit rates, in other words, increased the amount she saved out of current income and so reduced her consumption.

Do Higher Interest Rates *Stimulate* or *Reduce* Consumption?

This seemingly inverted relationship between interest rates and consumption seems to be borne out by recent empirical research. For example, Malhar Nabar, an economist at the IMF, tried in 2011 to measure the impact of changes in the real deposit rate on changes in Chinese consumptions levels. His conclusions are as follows:

> Panel estimates suggest that household savings respond strongly to a change in the real interest rate. A one percentage point increase in the real rate of return on bank deposits lowers the urban household saving rate by 0.6 percentage points.
>
> A comparison of the relationship across sub-periods shows that the association is stronger in the later period, 2003–09, relative to the earlier period, 1996–2002. The relationship is robust to the inclusion of variables that proxy for other influences on saving such as life cycle considerations and self-insurance against income volatility.
>
> The evidence also indicates that when the return on alternative investment is high (for example when real property price growth is relatively strong), a decline in the real return on bank deposits does not have as negative an impact on household portfolios.
>
> The results suggest that China's households save to meet a multiplicity of needs—retirement consumption, purchase of durables, self-insurance against income volatility and health shocks—and act as though they have a target level of saving in mind. An increase in financial rates of return, which raises the return on saving, makes it easier for them to meet their target saving. Financial reform that boosts interest rates could therefore have a strong effect on current tendencies to save.[3]

Chinese households, in other words, consume more (and save less) when real interest rates rise and do the opposite when real interest rates decline.

All this may seem counterintuitive for someone who assumes that what happens in the United States economy is "natural," but in fact it makes a great deal of sense. Financial repression is a tax that transfers resources from households, as net savers, to manufacturers, infrastructure investors, real estate developers, and others that generate economic activity.

This tax on households reduces consumption because it reduces disposable income, and the subsidy to borrowers (producers) increases the output of goods and services. As the gap between total production and total consumption rises, then by definition the savings rate must rise. If savings rise faster than investment, the trade surplus must rise. In that sense the financial repression tax is no different from the currency undervaluation tax or the lagging wage growth tax, except that the taxes are paid by a different set of households in each case and delivered to a different set of producers in each case.

Once again it is worth stressing that the changes in Chinese savings rate were affected by the central bank's setting of the deposit rate. They did not require changes in Chinese attitudes toward thrift and were wholly uninfluenced by cultural factors. The savings rate of Chinese households adjusted automatically to changes in underlying policy. And it is also worth stressing once again that these policies, which are not normally thought of as trade policies, inevitably must have an impact on a country's trade and its trade balance. There are in other words many ways that policies can affect trade, and not all of them are at first obvious.

And this is what might cause confusion, and often does, about the impact of specific trade-related policies. If one set of policies that affect trade in an obvious way is changed, we might not see the expected result because another set of less obvious policies may also be changed in the opposite way. For example, if a country decided to revalue its currency, but, worried about the impact that a declining trade surplus might have on domestic unemployment, reduced interest rates to spur domestic growth, it is very possible that the net impact on the trade surplus would be the opposite of what we expected.

Currency versus Interest Rates

How? If Japan raises the value of the yen, as it did after the Plaza Accords in 1985, but simultaneously increases credit expansion and lowers interest rates, as it also did, the positive impact on household consumption of the former can easily be overwhelmed by the negative impact of the latter. Revaluing the yen reduced the transfer from household income to the tradable goods sector, but expanding credit at lower real rates increased the transfer from households to net borrowers.

Because the latter impact exceeded the former, rather than decline, total savings actually rose in Japan, in which case the trade surplus also had to increase, allowing confused analysts to argue, very erroneously, that the empirical evidence showed no relationship between yen revaluation and trade rebalancing.

The same mistake is made regularly about China. An article in early 2012 shows how common this mistake is. According to the writer,

> China does not gain a big export advantage from Beijing's control of the yuan's exchange rate. Much of China's manufacturing industry consists of assembling components made elsewhere. The best example of this is Apple's iPods and iPads, which are treated as Chinese exports although only 5 per cent of their retail value is attributable to China. Virtually all of this trade is denominated in U.S. dollars, which means that any advantage China could have in export pricing is lost as a disadvantage on import pricing of the necessary components. The only real yuan-denominated input is assembly labour and this is a small proportion of total cost.
>
> The exchange rate record demonstrates the hollowness of the cheating claim. The yuan has gained 24 per cent against the U.S. dollar since it was allowed to strengthen in 2005, enough to dent any export advantage, and yet American complaints remain unchanged as if nothing had happened, which is, in effect, true. The yuan's exchange rate makes little difference.[4]

This argument may seem at first like robust common sense, but it is almost wholly mistaken. If the yuan's exchange rate really makes no difference to Chinese exports and imports, the correct and obvious conclusion cannot be that China should not revalue. On the contrary, it means that China should revalue immediately and substantially in order to improve its terms of trade at no cost to domestic employment. This should be obvious, but apparently it isn't.

Strangely enough Apple products seem to pop up in every article denying the impact of real factors on trade balances, but contrary to the author's claim they are most certainly not the best example of Chinese exports. The only reason they show up as "typical" examples in every article is precisely because they are so atypical and represent such an extreme case of assembly value added. Perhaps there should be a moratorium declared on the use of Apple products as a typical example of global trade. Most international trade does not consist of Apple products.

But the real mistakes here are the same two mistakes repeated over and over in literally hundreds of similar articles. The first mistake is the assumption that changes in the value of the currency will impact trade only by affecting the prices of the various components. This is not true—as we showed in chapter 2, changes in the value of the currency affect the trade balance by shifting income from one group within the country to another, and so changing the domestic savings rate. The share of imported inputs in the final product is slightly relevant to the extent that it affects disposable household income, and is generally negligible.

The second mistake is the claim that because the renminbi has appreciated by 24 percent since July 2005, without eliminating the trade imbalances, clearly the currency does not matter. If it did matter, goes the argument, the appreciation since 2005 would have resolved the dispute.

There are two serious problems with this argument. The first is to assume that any nominal increase in the value of the currency is equal to a real increase. It isn't. Since 2005 productivity has grown faster in China than in the United States, so the renminbi would have to rise by that differential— several percent annually—just to maintain its real relative value.

But a grosser mistake is to assume that the impact of the currency revaluation cannot be undermined by an expansion of credit at repressed interest rates, or by a reduction in real interest rates. In fact both happened in China after 2005, and their cumulative impact overwhelmed any change in the real value of the renminbi. When China began allowing the exchange value of the renminbi to rise after July 2005, it acted to counterbalance the employment impact by lowering the real interest rate and expanding credit dramatically.

More credit at lower interest rates increased the transfer from households to borrowers more rapidly than real appreciation in the currency (to the extent there was any) reduced the transfer from households to the tradable goods sector, and the net impact was that household consumption declined further and the national savings rate rose. In China, as in many other countries, the distortions created by financial repression are far greater than any distortion created by the currency.

CHAPTER FOUR

The Case of Unbalanced Growth in China

China in recent years has generated what is probably the largest trade surplus as a share of global GDP in history. Although many analysts describe this as evidence of a very successful growth model in which the trade surplus derives from good planning and fundamental strengths within the Chinese economy, it turns out that the Chinese trade surplus is actually a symptom of very distorted and unsustainable domestic policies, the reversal of which will be fraught with difficulty. It is a mistake to characterize China as an export-driven economy. China is an investment-driven economy. The trade surplus is a residual result of investment-related policies that force up the savings rate to levels above the investment rate.

S O FAR WE HAVE BEEN DISCUSSING the factors that affect trade balances in fairly abstract terms, so it might be useful to look at a specific case of a country with a number of policies in place that force up the national savings rate and, with it, a trade surplus. China, as is well known, has in the past decade experienced the largest trade surplus in the word, and as a share of global GDP its trade surplus may be the highest—or certainly among the highest—ever generated in history.

But China also has an extraordinarily high investment rate, the highest in the world, and this is something that is in principle unlikely to be accompanied by a high trade surplus. After all the current account surplus is exactly equal to the excess of savings over investment, and any country with an extraordinarily high investment rate should naturally run a current account deficit, as domestic savings are insufficient to exceed domestic investment. But China runs a huge current account surplus. This implies that China must also have an exceptionally high savings rate—one high enough fully to satisfy domestic needs and yet with enough excess to generate a very large surplus.

In fact China does have an extraordinarily high savings rate, and in this chapter we consider the reasons for such high savings. Before going further it is important to note that an excessively high savings rate can be just as debilitating for an economy, perhaps even more so, as an excessively low savings rate.

Many analysts find this hard to believe. There is a tendency for analysts to be overly U.S.-centric when considering economic conditions in China and many other countries—and this is a problem not just among American and other non-Chinese analysts, but even among Chinese analysts. The United States clearly suffers from a low savings rate, and the consequences of a low savings rate are widely understood, so analysts tend to assume that only low savings can be a problem, whereas on the other hand high savings must be a good thing and extraordinarily high savings must be an extraordinarily good thing.

But this is not the case. In fact as we saw in chapter 1, excessively high global savings were central to the speculative capital flows and trade imbalances that led to the global crisis, and countries like China were at the heart of the savings excess. China's very unbalanced economy—unbalanced in the opposite way of that of the United States and in an even more extreme form—has generated its own internal problems—very different from the problems in the United States—and this is an important part of the story of trade imbalances. Unfortunately the analysis in the previous two chapters suggests that it might be even more difficult for a country like China to adjust to a rebalanced world economy than it will be for the United States.

It is worth stepping back briefly to understand the domestic problems created by these imbalances and to note for how long these problems have been apparent. On the morning of March 16, 2007, in Beijing's Great Hall of the People, Wen Jiabao, China's premier at the time, held a press conference just before the end of the Fifth Session of the Tenth National People's Congress. After questions from reporters from several different media organizations, including the *Wall Street Journal*, the *People's Daily*, China's CCTV, *Le Monde*, and the *Financial Times*, a reporter from *China News Service* asked the premier the kind of question that should have been a layup:

> China's growth rate has exceeded 10% while the inflation rate has been kept below 3% for four years running. This is rare both in China and the world. Some scholars believe that China's economy will reach a turning point in 2007. What's your view? What do you think are the major problems in China's economy? Will China be able to maintain such a momentum of high growth and low inflation?[1]

Premier Wen's response was surprisingly frank, and his characterization of the economy caused a sensation:

> China's economy has maintained fast yet steady growth in recent years. However, this gives no cause for complacency, neither in the past, nor now, or in the future. My mind is focused on the pressing challenges. "A country that appears peaceful and stable may encounter unexpected crises." There are structural problems in China's economy which cause unsteady, unbalanced, uncoordinated and unsustainable development.

Within minutes of his ending the press conference headlines flashed around the world proclaiming that Premier Wen had called China's development "unsteady, unbalanced, uncoordinated and unsustainable." This was the strongest possible confirmation of what skeptics had long been arguing—China's growth model was seriously lopsided and for all its seeming success could be storing important adjustment problems for the future.

Premier Wen went on to elaborate what he meant by those words:

> Unsteady development means overheated investment as well as excessive credit supply and liquidity and surplus in foreign trade and international payments. Unbalanced development means uneven development

between urban and rural areas, between different regions and between economic and social development. Uncoordinated development means that there is lack of proper balance between the primary, secondary and tertiary sectors and between investment and consumption. Economic growth is mainly driven by investment and export. Unsustainable development means that we have not done well in saving energy and resources and protecting the environment. All these are pressing problems facing us, which require long-term efforts to resolve.

I have said that China's economy has enjoyed fast yet steady growth for years. Can we sustain this momentum? First, the conditions are there. The most important condition is that we have a fairly long peaceful international environment that enables us to focus on economic development. Second, we have a domestic market with huge potential. However, the key to sustaining the momentum of China's economic growth lies in our ability to pursue the right policies.

We will continue to expand domestic demand, especially consumption. We will press ahead with reform and opening up to remove institutional and structural obstacles and enhance knowledge and technology based innovation. All this will lay down a solid foundation for ensuring economic growth. We will further promote energy and resources saving and reduction of pollutant discharge to make economic growth sustainable. The task is a difficult one, but we are confident that we can accomplish it.

For the next several days and weeks commentators applauded the premier's forthrightness and discussed the meaning of the phrase "unsteady, unbalanced, uncoordinated and unsustainable." This, however, was not the last time Premier Wen was to worry publicly. Two and a half years later when it seemed to many, even though the imbalances signaled by Wen had all gotten worse, that China had managed altogether to sidestep the global crisis, on September 10, 2009, in a speech at the World Economic Forum in Dalian, a city in northeastern China, Premier Wen made a very similar claim. "China's economic rebound," he told the attendees, "is unstable, unbalanced and not yet solid."

And within the most senior policymaking circles it was not just Wen Jiabao who worried. In June 2010, writing in the government-owned *Qiu Shi* magazine, Vice Premier Li Keqiang—who was anointed the next premier after the change in leadership in late 2012—said that China's past development has created an "irrational economic structure" and "uncoordinated and unsustainable development is increasingly apparent."

He added that China's long-term dependence on investment and exports for growth "will grow the instability of the economy." During 2010 and 2011 rumors swept the community of China-watching economists that Li was pressing for interest rate increases and other steps necessary to force a more rapid adjustment, but given the lack of consensus and the risks associated with the leadership change, he had not been able to get his way.

For the rest of 2011 and 2012, even with the great reluctance among policymakers to take strong and possibly controversial stands during a once-in-a-decade leadership transition period, the debate about rebalancing became louder. In September 2011 at the World Economic Forum in Dalian, professor Zhang Weiying, former dean of the very prestigious Guanghua School of Peking University, China's most reputable university, lambasted the inability of the leadership to manage the pace of reform. He described the very powerful National Development and Reform Commission, the bureaucrats who produce and manage the country's economic blueprints, as "a bunch of smart people doing something really stupid."[2]

It has become a contentious debate. Proponents of one form of rebalancing, which involved significant political and economic liberalization, fought for what was often referred to in the press as the "Guangdong model," versus the more statist "Chongqing model," which would, perhaps a little mysteriously, also deliver rebalancing of the economy but under stricter state control and preferably through the leadership of the "revolutionary" families. In early 2012 an astonishing series of events resulted in the deposition of Bo Xilai as mayor of Chongqing and the presumed leader of "Chongqing model" faction that opposed significant reforms.

For many commentators Bo Xilai's downfall, he was subsequently suspended from the twenty-five-person Politburo in April, had to do mainly with his unseemly populist behavior in attempting to force himself into the nine-man Standing Committee, the most senior policymaking body in China. But a more plausible explanation was that his downfall was simply part of the contentious debate—although an especially colorful part—between reformers and antireformers, and it should not have been unexpected.

Most political commentators believe the debate will continue after the leadership change as the reformers try to build a consensus for what is sure to be a difficult transition period. The difficulty is that any rebalancing will require, by definition, an inversion of the relative growth rates of the state and household sectors. This will not be easy. For the past decade, as China grew by 10–12 percent annually, household income grew by 7–8 percent annually while the state sector grew by nearly 15 percent annually.

Rebalancing will require, as I demonstrate in the rest of this chapter, that household income grow faster than GDP, and so by definition the state sector must grow more slowly. Even if we accept what I believe are excessively optimistic average annual growth expectations of 7 percent for the next decade, for China to rebalance, the average growth rate of the state sector cannot exceed 5 percent annually (and I believe GDP growth rates will be much lower than 7 percent). The transition from a state in which the accumulation of state assets grows by roughly 15 percent or more annually to one in which it grows by less than 5 percent will be at the heart of the distributional struggles among Chinese factions and prominent Chinese families.

What Kind of Imbalance?

Is China's growth "unbalanced," and if so, in what sense is it unbalanced, and how does that affect the trade account? Most commentators pretty much agree that China's economy is indeed unbalanced, and they agree on the nature of the fundamental imbalances. Chinese growth is unbalanced because the very rapid GDP growth generated especially in the past decade has relied too heavily on net exports and investment and too little on domestic household consumption. The most striking expression of this imbalance is the declining share of GDP represented by household consumption.

The story of Chinese consumption since the 1978 reforms is instructive. In the 1980s household consumption represented about 50 to 52 percent of GDP. This is not an unprecedented number, but it is very low. Consumption for most European countries lies in the 60 to 65 percent range. Consumption for other developing countries can easily fall in the 65 to 70 percent range—within which range much of Latin America lies. Consumption in the United States has been around 70 to 72 percent in recent years.

By Asian standards, however, Chinese consumption in the 1980s was not exceptionally low. South Korean and Malaysian consumption is around 50 to 55 percent of GDP (although during and after the Asian crisis Malaysian consumption did drop to around 45 percent of GDP, before recovering after a year). Other major Asian economies, like India, Japan, Taiwan, and Thailand, show consumption in the 55 to 60 percent of GDP range.

Nonetheless, even though it started the decade at the low end of the range even for low-consuming Asian countries, as the country grew during the 1990s Chinese consumption declined further as a share of GDP. By the end of the decade Chinese household consumption represented a meager 46 percent of GDP. This was not unprecedented—Malaysian consumption after all had dropped to 45 percent a year after the 1997 crisis—but the Chinese consumption level was more typical of a country in crisis than of a country in ruddy good health.

But the story doesn't end there. By 2005 household consumption in China had declined to around 40 percent of GDP. With the exception of a few very special and unique cases, this level is unprecedented in modern economic history. Beijing's response to this very low number, not surprisingly, was a worried one. Policymakers pledged during 2005 to take every step necessary to raise household consumption growth and to help rebalance the economy.

Why were they worried? Because, as we pointed out in chapter 1, in any economy there are three sources of demand—domestic consumption, domestic investment, and the trade surplus—which together compose total demand, or GDP. If a country has a very low domestic consumption share, by definition it is overly reliant on domestic investment and the trade surplus to generate growth.

This meant that future Chinese growth was vulnerable. Policymakers, of course, cannot fully control the trade surplus because this depends on the ability and willingness of the rest of the world to continue absorbing China's deficient demand. With the largest trade surplus ever recorded as a share of global GDP—all the more astounding given that the two previous record holders, Japan in the late 1980s and the United States in the late 1920s, were countries whose share of global GDP was two to three times China's share—it wasn't at all obvious that China could expect its trade surplus to increase much more.

Furthermore there was also already a great deal of concern that China's high investment rate was proving unsustainable. Beijing had engineered for China extremely high and growing investment rates for the previous twenty-five years, and this made a great deal of economic sense at the beginning of the reform process, after 1978, when China was seriously and obviously underinvested for its level of social development. But after so many years of furious investment growth, there were increasing worries that China had become overinvested, perhaps even massively overinvested, by the early and middle part of the decade.

We will more fully discuss China's vulnerability to the trade surplus and investment later in this chapter, but with consumption so low, it would mean that China was overly reliant for growth on two sources of demand that were unsustainable and hard to control. Only by shifting to higher domestic consumption could the country reduce its vulnerability and ensure continued rapid growth. This is why in 2005, with household consumption at a shockingly low 40 percent of GDP, Beijing announced its resolve to rebalance the economy toward a greater consumption share.

Not surprisingly most observers, both foreign and Chinese, hailed Beijing's new resolve to raise the consumption share of GDP and excitedly reported that with these new initiatives the problem of a too-low household consumption share was about to be addressed and fixed. There was a widespread perception that Beijing had always managed to achieve its economic targets in the past, and this new economic target would also be dispatched with efficiency.

A few economists, however, were very skeptical. They pointed out that previous policy successes had almost always involved targets that could be resolved mainly by increases in investment. The real lesson, they argued, was not that Beijing was able to manage the economy efficiently and intelligently; it was that Beijing was able to increase investment whenever it wanted. Given low transparency, limited political accountability, and near-total control over national savings and the banking system, perhaps this should not have been a surprise.

Rebalancing the economy toward consumption, however, could not be achieved by mandating higher investment. On the contrary, it would require lower investment. This, the skeptics argued, would make the target much harder to achieve because when it came to achieving economic targets that could not be met simply by increasing investment, it was not clear that Beijing had ever been very effective.

They further argued that a low and declining consumption share of GDP was not an accident; it was fundamental to the growth model. China did not grow quickly, in other words, *in spite* of lagging consumption growth—it grew quickly *because* of lagging consumption growth. In that case Beijing would not be able to raise the consumption share of GDP easily because doing so would require abandoning the investment-driven growth model altogether, and there was as of yet no political consensuses in favor of taking the necessary drastic steps. They warned that consumption would barely grow from the 40 percent level for many years and might even stagnate further.

It turned out that even the skeptics underestimated the difficulty of the adjustment China was facing. For the next five years GDP growth continued to surge ahead of household consumption growth until by 2010, the last year for which we have complete statistics as of this writing, household consumption declined to an astonishing 34 percent of GDP. This level is almost surreal. For all its determination, in other words, not only was Beijing wholly incapable of reversing the downward trend in the household consumption share of GDP, it could not even prevent a near collapse.

The flip side of the decline in consumption of course has been the rise in savings, which is simply the obverse of consumption. Part of the rise in savings has been the rise in household savings. After bouncing around erratically between 10 percent and 20 percent of disposable income in the 1980s, by 1990 Chinese household savings equaled 12–15 percent of disposable income. Around 1992 household savings began rising steadily until 1998, and then stabilized at around 24–25 percent until very recently, when they rose slightly to about 26 percent of disposable income.

Growth Miracles Are Not New

But this is not the whole story—household savings are only part of total national savings. The real increase in national savings in recent years was caused by the sharp increase in corporate and government savings, although it is worth pointing out that corporate savings, and even government savings, are themselves caused by the transfer from household savings via low interest rates and other hidden transfers, as we will see later. Corporate and governments savings, in other words, were savings effectively imposed on the household sector.

During this three-decade period China ran small surpluses or deficits on the trade account from 1978 until 1996, when it booked its last trade deficit, beginning thereafter a steady upward march of its trade surplus until 2003, when the trade surplus was around 5 percent of China's GDP. After 2003, China's trade surplus surged, to reach over 10 percent of GDP in 2007–8, before coming down sharply in 2009 and 2010 as a result of the global crisis in demand.

Investment, too, rose steadily during this period as a share of GDP, as indeed it had to if the growth model was going to work. In 1990 it was around 23 percent of GDP. It rose sharply in 1992–94 to around 31 percent of GDP, stabilized at that level, and then began climbing inexorably around 1997–98 to reach 50 percent in 2011, and even more if we include, as we should, imported commodities that are stockpiled (rising inventories are a form of investment).

Rising investment, rising savings, and rising trade surpluses are inextricably linked in China's case, and nothing suggests how impressive was the increase in China's national savings rate as the fact that China was able to combine a soaring investment rate with a soaring trade surplus. Because, as we showed in chapter 1, the trade surplus is a function of the excess of savings over investment, normally a high and soaring investment rate should be associated with a declining trade surplus, or even (and more normally) a large and rising trade deficit.

This is what happened, for example, in the United States during the nineteenth century, when very high domestic investment rates exceeded domestic savings, and the United States had to import foreign capital, mostly from Great Britain and the Netherlands, for most of the century. As the obverse, of course, the United States also ran trade deficits for most of the nineteenth century. Yet China, with an even higher investment rate, one of the highest in history, was able nonetheless to run an extraordinarily high trade surplus. The only way this could happen is if the savings rate was even more extraordinarily high.

And it was, but why? We have already discussed the many policies, ranging from undervalued currencies, to lagging wag growth, to financial repression, to environmental degradation and weakening social safety nets as policies or institutional structures that encouraged very rapid growth but at the expense of the household share of that growth. All of these occurred in China to an exaggerated extent, and it was for these reasons that Chinese savings soared.

These growth strategies engineered by Beijing forced households to subsidize investment and production, thus generating rapid economic and employment growth at the expense of household income growth. It is the lagging growth in household income, as we showed in the previous two chapters, that has primarily constrained household consumption growth.

This is borne out by the numbers. From 1990 to 2002, household income ranged from 64 percent of GDP to 72 percent of GDP. It peaked in 1992, before a tremendous bout of inflation in 1993 and 1994 brought it down, and then began a slow, erratic descent to 66 percent in 2002, after which time it plunged to under 50 percent of GDP, if the numbers can be believed (most analysts assume that there is substantial hidden income in China, especially among the wealthy and very wealthy, that is not captured in the official surveys).[3]

If there were a way to measure changes in wealth—for example the value of the deteriorating social safety nets and the degrading environment, the present value of savings as interest rates are changed for policy reasons, etc.—and household income were adjusted by these changes, the decline in household wealth relative to GDP would have probably been even greater. Certainly that is what the savings numbers imply.

But with Chinese household consumption and household income growing so rapidly in the past decade, around 7–8 percent annually, why has it been so difficult to raise the consumption share of GDP and reduce China's overwhelming dependence on a growing trade surplus and especially accelerating investment to generate growth? In order to understand the causes of China's great imbalance it is necessary to consider the development model that generated its tremendous growth in the past two decades.

There is nothing especially Chinese about the Chinese development model. It is mostly a souped-up version of the Asian development model, probably first articulated by Japan in the 1960s, and shares fundamental features with a number of periods of rapid growth—for example Germany during the 1930s, Brazil during the "miracle" years of the 1960s and 1970, and the Soviet Union in the 1950s and 1960s, when most informed opinion (including, apparently, President Kennedy) expected the country to overtake the United States economically well before the end of the century. While these policies can generate tremendous growth early on, they also lead inexorably to deep imbalances.

At the heart of the various models are massive subsidies for manufacturing and investment aimed at generating rapid growth and the building up of infrastructure and manufacturing capacity. These subsidies make it very cheap to increase investment in manufacturing capacity, infrastructure, and real estate development, generating enormous growth in employment, and they allow investors, whether private or, more typically, the state, to generate great profitability.

The Brazilian Miracle

But of course, as we showed in chapters 2 and 3, all subsidies must be paid for by someone, and in nearly every case they are paid for by the household sector. In some cases, as with the Brazilian investment-driven miracle in the 1960s and 1970s, the household costs are explicit. Brazil taxed household income heavily and invested the proceeds in manufacturing and infrastructure. In doing this it managed to achieve eye-popping growth rates. As MIT professor Yasheng Huang put it tantalizingly in a *Wall Street Journal* piece,

> Guess which country boasted the following characteristics: GDP grew at 11% annually for almost 10 years. The authoritarian, one-party state promoted rapid industrialization by relocating workers to coastal urban areas. The government welcomed foreign-direct investment and courted companies through tax exemptions and other benefits. Seventy-five percent of the top 100 largest domestic firms' assets belonged to the state sector. The government's savings rate doubled in less than a decade, while the agricultural share of employment fell by more than one-third over the same period.[4]

Of course Huang was talking not about China but about Brazil from 1965 to 1974, during which time it may have been the first country to which the term "economic miracle" was applied to describe the astonishing growth surge. That miracle was achieved by using high levels of income tax to confiscate household wealth and use the proceeds not to improve social benefits but rather simply to subsidize the ferocious spurt of growth.

This is not necessarily a bad strategy. Brazil achieved extraordinary growth, and with it, income levels rose quickly. But as the history of every investment-driven growth miracle, including that of Brazil, shows, high levels of state-directed subsidized investment run an increasing risk of being misallocated, and the longer this goes on the more wealth is likely to be destroyed even as the economy posts high GDP growth rates. The difference between posted GDP growth rates and real increases in wealth shows up as excess debt. Eventually the imbalances this misallocation creates have to be resolved, and the wealth destruction has to be recognized as debt levels are paid down.

With such heavy distortions imposed and maintained by the central government, there was no easy way for the economy to adjust on its own. Growth was not capable of being sustained except by rising debt, and by the mid-1970s Brazil reached its domestic debt capacity limit, as loans simply could not be repaid out of earnings. Fortunately for the administration of President Ernesto Geisel—but unfortunately for Brazil—the contraction of domestic debt capacity coincided with the petrodollar crisis, in which international banks had to recycle soaring dollar earnings from OPEC nations with few opportunities to deploy these earnings in Europe and the United States, which were then suffering from economic stagnation.

The petrodollars were recycled in massive amounts in developing countries, including miracle-growth Brazil, that were able to continue funding high levels of wasteful investment and maintain GDP growth, even with the oil price shocks of the 1970s, at nearly 6 percent. But of course excess debt continued to rise. Because the external funding too had its limits, by 1981–82 after the accompanying debt levels proved to be a limit to further expansion, Brazil spent much of the 1980s, its famous Lost Decade, reversing the growth that occurred during its miracle years. Debt, as we will learn over the next few years in China, has always been the Achilles' heel of the investment-driven growth model.

There are however some important differences among forms of the investment-driven growth model. The Asian or Japanese variety relies on less explicit taxation mechanisms to accomplish the same purpose of subsidizing investment. Rather than confiscating household wealth through high income taxes, as the Brazilian version of the model did, three much more indirect mechanisms are used for the same effect, as we discussed in chapter 3.

First, wage growth is constrained to well below the growth in worker productivity. In China, for example, worker productivity has grown much faster than wages, especially during the past decade, during which time workers' wages have slightly more than doubled, while productivity has nearly tripled.

There are many reasons for the gap between the two. One reason, as we also discussed in chapter 3, may have to do with the huge pool of surplus labor in the countryside available to compete for jobs and so keep wages low. There are also other, policy-related reasons that limit wage growth. Workers are not able to organize except in government-sponsored unions that more often see things from the point of view of employers than from that of workers. Migrant workers are also unable to get residence permits, called *hukou*, and without *hukou* what limited protection workers may have is sharply reduced because living in an urban area without the proper *hukou* is tolerated but technically illegal.

The important thing to remember from the growth model perspective is that, whatever the reason, lagging wage growth in China represented a transfer of wealth from workers to employers. An increasing share of whatever workers produced, in other words, accrued to employers, and this effective subsidy allowed employers to generate transferred profit or to cover real losses. The fact that productivity grew much faster than wages acted like a growing tax on workers' wages, the proceeds of which went to subsidize employers.

And remember the impact this hidden tax has on the relationship between GDP growth and household income growth, as we discussed in chapter 3. By effectively subsidizing employers at the expense of workers, it boosted the competitivity of businesses, and increased overall production, while constraining household income, and with it, household consumption. This forced up China's savings rate.

The second mechanism common among Asian development model countries for transferring income from households to manufacturers, as we also have already discussed, is an undervalued exchange rate, and most analysts acknowledged that after the massive devaluation of the renminbi in 1994, followed by soaring productivity (which increased the real undervaluation of a currency), the renminbi was seriously undervalued for much of the past two decades.

It is not wholly meaningful to discuss by how much the renminbi was undervalued because any undervaluation of the currency must be considered in conjunction with the other transfers that had similar impacts on the trade balance. Most economists, however, have estimated the undervaluation to be anywhere from 15 percent to 30 percent, which given long-term changes in productivity and inflation is probably a reasonable if imprecise estimate.

Powering Growth

Clearly this represents a significant undervaluation. The undervaluation of the exchange rate, remember, is a kind of consumption tax imposed on all imported goods, and everyone in China who is a net importer, which includes all households except perhaps subsistence farmers, must pay this very large implicit tax.

On the other hand Chinese manufacturers in the tradable goods sector, heavily concentrated in Guangdong and the coastal provinces, receive the opposite "negative" tax, or subsidy, in the form of lower domestic costs relative to higher foreign prices for their goods. Again we must remember the impact this hidden consumption tax has on the relationship between GDP growth and household income growth. By raising the cost of foreign imports, it puts downward pressure on real household income in China.

But by subsidizing Chinese exporters, thus increasing their competitive strengths relative to foreign competitors, the undervaluation of the renminbi boosts domestic production. An undervalued exchange rate is simply another powerful mechanism for increasing the gap between what a country produces and what it consumes, and this forces up the savings rate, not only affecting the trade account, as we showed in chapter 2, but with high GDP growth being created through high investment growth, an undervalued currency also creates domestic imbalances in the way growth is generated.

The third mechanism for creating the domestic imbalances, and probably by far the most powerful, as we discussed in chapter 3, is financial repression. The Chinese financial system is, or has been until very recently, severely repressed. Almost all household savings in China are in the form of bank deposits, and the banks are controlled by the monetary authorities, who determine the direction of credit, socialize the risks, and set interest rates.

In China, the central bank, the People's Bank of China, following instructions of the State Council, sets both the maximum deposit rate, above which banks cannot pay, and the minimum lending rate, below which banks cannot lend. Because it sets both rates very low, it is effectively transferring a large share of resources from depositors to borrowers.

How large a share? In the past decade nominal lending rates have averaged little more than 6 percent even as the economy grew nominally by 14 to 15 percent annually. Even if we accept that annual GDP growth has been overstated by 2 or 3 percentage points,[5] this still implies that borrowers received a hugely disproportionate share of growth at the expense of depositors. With lending rates 4 to 7 percentage points below adjusted GDP growth rates, and with household deposits (including farm deposits) equal to anywhere from 80 percent to 100 percent of GDP, the total transfer from households to state-owned enterprises, infrastructure investors, and other favored institutions amounts to anywhere from 3 percent to 8 percent of GDP annually.

In addition, in China, as in many of the countries that followed the Asian development model, not only have interest rates been set extremely low, but the minimum spread between the deposit rate and the lending rate is set very high, thereby guaranteeing the banks a large, and very safe, profit. This also comes at the expense of depositors. Using the same methodology as above, we can estimate the additional transfers to be roughly equal 1 percent of GDP. In a country where household income accounts for approximately 50 percent of GDP, these combined interest-rate-related transfers, of 4 to 9 percent of GDP, represent a very high hidden tax on households.

Depositors, however, cannot opt out. There are significant restrictions on their ability to take capital out of the country, and for the most part only the very rich can exploit these opportunities. Nor are there many domestic investment opportunities. Local stock and bond markets are rudimentary, highly speculative, and rife with insider activity—which effectively transfers profits from noninsiders to insiders while leaving the former with the full risk.

There are few other legal and safe alternatives to the banking system. The most common alternatives include real estate and the so-called informal banking sector, both of which generally have very high transaction costs and limited liquidity, so neither is a useful investment alternative for depositors with limited means or who may need to be able to access their savings quickly.

Depositors, in other words, have little choice but to accept very low deposit rates on their savings, which are then transferred through the banking system to banks and borrowers who benefit from these very low rates. Very low lending and deposit rates create a powerful mechanism for using household savings to boost growth by heavily subsidizing the cost of capital.

And remember yet again the impact this hidden tax on savings has on the relationship between GDP growth and household income growth. By lowering borrowing costs substantially, it encourages investment primarily in real estate development, infrastructure building, and of course manufacturing capacity (in China there is very little consumer financing).

But by reducing the amount of interest income depositors receive, it reduces the overall income they should be earning, and this is especially noticeable in a country where savings are so high and income so low as a share of GDP. This is certainly a powerful mechanism for increasing the gap between what a country produces and what it consumes. It also forces up the savings rate dramatically.

As an aside, the resulting low, or even negative, cost of capital for Chinese borrowers explains the seeming paradox of China's capital-intensive, rather than labor-intensive, growth. Ask most people what China's comparative advantage is, and they are likely to say that it is the huge pool of cheap and disciplined labor. But in fact this doesn't seem to be reflected in the economy. If China's comparative advantage were cheap labor, we would expect its growth to be heavily labor intensive as businesses loaded up on the most efficient input.

But China's growth is actually heavily capital intensive. It is in fact among the most capital intensive in the world and far more so than any other developing country—even countries that are far richer and with far higher wage levels. Chinese businesses behave, in other words, not as if labor were the cheapest input they have but rather as if capital were the cheapest input. They are right. Labor may be cheap, but capital is free. It may even have a negative cost.

Paying for Subsidies

All three of these mechanisms do the same thing, albeit by distributing the costs and benefits in different ways to different groups among households and producers. They effectively tax household income and use the proceeds to subsidize producers, infrastructure investors, real estate developers, local and provincial borrowers, central government borrowers—in fact anyone who has access to bank lending, who employs workers, or who manufactures tradable goods, whether or not they actually export them.

In principle these mechanisms are no different from mechanisms used by the Brazilians during their "miracle" years. Brasília heavily taxed household income and used the proceeds to promote industrialization and growth. Beijing does the same thing, but the taxes are hidden. The only real difference is that after 1975–76, when domestic borrowing capacity had become constrained, Brazil turned to external financing—subsidized by government guarantees—to fund investment, and so the impact of net foreign capital inflows meant that Brazil exported a portion of its domestic demand through a current account deficit—which perhaps accounts for the slowdown in growth relative to the early miracle years.

Besides the ones we have discussed, there are many other such hidden taxes in China. To repeat from an earlier chapter, environmental degradation, a serious problem with China's growth model, is an important transfer of income from households to businesses. Likewise energy and water subsidies (including the cost of building facilities), the deterioration in the social safety net once provided by work units, subsidized land sales, ease of eminent domain expropriations, and so on are all forms of tax and subsidy.

Not surprisingly, these enormous transfers have made it very profitable for governments, businesses, and real estate developers to invest in infrastructure and productive capacity, even if the real returns on the projects did not justify the costs. In so doing they ignited an investment boom.

The result of this enormously successful model is so much investment-driven and employment-generating growth that even with massive transfers from households, household income has nonetheless surged. In China, for the past decade, as the country was clocking in growth rates of 10–11 percent annually, household income, and with it household consumption, grew 7–9 percent annually.

In a sense it seems like a free lunch. Household income is taxed heavily in order to generate tremendous growth. This growth causes employment to surge, and as workers move from subsistence living in rural China to the factories and development sites of the cities, their income surges. So rapidly does household income grow that even after the huge hidden taxes are deducted the wealth and ability to consume of the average Chinese grows at a pace that is the envy of world. So why not continue this growth model forever?

In fact there are very strong arguments in favor of versions of this growth model followed by Brazil, China, and many others. Alexander Gerschenkron, the Ukrainian-born American economic historian, posited in the 1950s and 1960s the concept of "backwardness," and argued that the more backward an economy was at any point in time—with relatively low manufacturing capacity and infrastructure, and perhaps higher levels of social capital—the more growth could be generated under conditions in which consumption would be constrained in favor of investment and the savings rate forced up. He argued that because of failures in the private financial sector to identify investments with positive externalities, there was likely to be, and ought to be, a greater reliance on state-directed banks to allocate capital.[6]

In a 2003 article Columbia University economist Albert Fishlow further elucidated Gerschenkron's position:

1. Relative backwardness creates a tension between the promise of economic development, as achieved elsewhere, and the continuity of stagnation. Such a tension takes political form and motivates institutional innovation, whose product becomes appropriate substitution for the absent preconditions for growth.

2. The greater the degree of backwardness, the more intervention is required in the market economy to channel capital and entrepreneurial leadership to nascent industries, also the more coercive and comprehensive are the measures required to reduce domestic consumption and allow national saving.

3. The more backward the economy, the more likely are a series of additional characteristics: an emphasis upon domestic production of producers' goods rather than consumers' goods; the use of capital-intensive rather than labor-intensive methods of production; emergence of larger-scale production units at both the firm level as well as the individual plant level; and dependence upon borrowed, advanced technology rather than use of indigenous techniques.

4. The more backward the country, the less likely the agricultural sector is to provide a growing market to industry, and the more dependent industry is upon growing productivity and interindustrial sales for its expansion. Such unbalanced growth is frequently made feasible through state participation.[7]

Limits to Backwardness

This sounds a lot like the Chinese growth model. In fact countries undergoing the process described by Gerschenkron were able to generate fairly substantial increases in wealth for long periods of time—as clearly happened in China, at least during the first fifteen or twenty years since the reforms of 1978. But the case of China, and every other case of an investment-driven growth miracle, suggests that the model cannot be sustained because there are at least two constraints. The first has to do with the constraint on debt-financed investment and the second with the constraint on the external account, and one or both constraints have always eventually derailed the growth model.

To address the first constraint, in the early stages for most countries that have followed the investment-driven growth model, when investment is low, the diversion of household wealth into investment in capacity and infrastructure is likely to be economically productive. After all, when capital stock per person is almost nonexistent, almost any increase in capital stock is likely to drive worker productivity higher. When you have no roads, even a simple dirt road will sharply increase the value of local labor.

The longer heavily subsidized investment continues, however, the more likely that cheap capital and socialized credit risk will fund economically wasteful projects. Dirt roads quickly become paved roads. Paved roads become highways. And highways become superhighways with eight lanes in either direction. The decision to upgrade is politically easy to make because each new venture generates local employment, rapid economic growth in the short term, and opportunities for fraud and what economists politely call rent-seeking behavior, while the costs are spread through the entire country through the banking system and over the many years during which the debt is repaid (and most debt is rolled over continuously).

It also seems easy to justify intellectually the infrastructure upgrades. After all, rich countries have far more capital stock per person than poor countries, and those investments were presumably economically justified, so, according to this way of thinking, it will take decades of continual upgrading before China comes close to overbuilding.

The problem with this reasoning of course is that it ignores the economic reason for upgrading capital stock and assumes that capital and infrastructure have the same value everywhere in the world. They don't. Worker productivity and wages are so much lower in China than in the developed world. This means that the economic value of infrastructure in China, which is based primarily on the value of wages it saves, is a fraction of the value of identical infrastructure in the developed world. It makes no economic sense, in other words, for China to have levels of infrastructure and capital stock anywhere near those of much richer countries because this would represent wasted resources—like exchanging cheap labor for much more expensive labor-saving devices.

Of course because risk is socialized—that is, all borrowing is implicitly or explicitly guaranteed by the state—no one needs to ask whether or not the locals can use the highway and whether the economic wealth created is enough to repay the cost. The system creates an acute form of what is sometimes called the "commonwealth" problem. The benefits of investment accrue over the immediate future and within the jurisdiction of the local leader who makes the investment decision.

The costs, however, are spread widely through the national banking system and over many years, during which time, presumably, the leader responsible for the investment will have been promoted to another post in another jurisdiction. With very low interest rates and other subsidies making it hard to determine whether investments actually reduce value or create it, the commonwealth problem ensures that further investment in infrastructure is always encouraged.

The problem of overinvestment is not just an infrastructure problem. It occurs just as easily in manufacturing. When manufacturers can borrow money at such a low rate that they effectively force most of the borrowing cost onto household depositors, they don't need to create economic value equal to or greater than the cost of the investment. Even factories that systematically destroy value can show high profits, and there is substantial evidence to suggest that the state-owned sector in the aggregate has probably been a massive value destroyer for most if not all the past decade, but is nonetheless profitable thanks to household subsidies.[8]

At some point, in other words, rather than creating wealth, capital users begin to destroy wealth, but nonetheless show profits by passing more than 100 percent of the losses onto households. The very cheap capital especially means that a very significant portion of the cost—as much as 20–40 percent of the total amount of the loan—is forced onto depositors just in the form of low interest rates.[9] This is effectively a form of debt forgiveness granted, unknowingly, by depositors.

Under these circumstances it would take heroic levels of restraint and understanding for investors not to engage in value-destroying activity. This is why countries following the investment-driven growth model—like Germany in the 1930s, the Soviet Union in the 1950s and 1960s, Brazil in the 1960s and 1970s, Japan in the 1980s, and many other smaller countries—have always overinvested for many years, leading, in every case, either to a debt crisis or a "lost decade" of surging debt and low growth.[10]

The Trade Impact

The second constraint is that policies that force households to subsidize growth are likely to generate much faster growth in production than in consumption—growth in household consumption being largely a function of household income growth. In that case even with high investment levels, large and growing trade surpluses are needed to absorb the balance because, as quickly as it is rising, the investment share of GDP still cannot increase quickly enough to absorb the decline in the consumption share.

This is what happened in China in the past decade until the crisis in 2007–8, after which Beijing had to engineer an extraordinary additional surge in investment in order to counteract the contraction in the current account surplus. As Chinese manufacturers created rapidly expanding amounts of goods, the transfers from the household sector needed to subsidize this rapid expansion in manufacturing left them unable to purchase a constant share of the goods being produced. The result was that China needed to export a growing share of what it produced, and this is exactly what it did, especially after 2003.

As long as the rest of the world—primarily the United States and the trade deficit countries of Europe and Latin America—have been able to absorb China's rising trade surplus, the fact that domestic households absorbed a declining share of Chinese production didn't matter much. A surge in American and European consumer financing allowed those countries to experience consumption growth that exceeded the growth in their own manufacture of goods and services.

But by 2007 China's trade surplus as a share of global GDP had become the highest recorded in one hundred years, perhaps ever, and the rest of the world found it increasing difficult to absorb it. To make matters worse, the global financial crisis sharply reduced the ability and willingness of other countries even to maintain current trade deficits, and as we will see this downward pressure on China's current account surplus is likely to continue.

So China has hit both constraints—capital is wasted, perhaps on an unprecedented scale, and the world is finding it increasingly difficult to absorb excess Chinese capacity—and in fact may have hit the former constraint a decade or more ago. For all its past success China now needs urgently to abandon the development model because debt is rising furiously and at an unsustainable pace, and once China reaches its debt capacity limits, perhaps in four or five years, growth will come crashing down.

The sooner it abandons the model the less painful the adjustment, but it will be difficult under any scenario, even with an immediate and sizable adjustment. China must raise wages, interest rates, and the value of the currency in order to reverse the flow of wealth from the household sector to the state and corporate sector, but if it does so quickly it could cause severe financial distress to businesses and projects heavily dependent on subsidized costs, and the resulting surge in unemployment could actually cause consumption to decline just as Chinese competitiveness abroad deteriorates.

If it does so slowly, on the other hand, China will need continued accommodation from the external sector, but it is not at all clear that the rest of the world, most importantly the United States and the trade deficit countries of Europe, will allow their trade deficits to stay high—in fact peripheral Europe has no choice but to see its deficits contract. What's more, a slow adjustment means the imbalances and debt will continue to get worse for several years before they get better, and during that time China will have to pile on ever more wasted investment to keep growth manageable.

A Lost Decade?

The historical precedents for this kind of adjustment are not encouraging, and the adjustment China needs to make dwarfs those of its predecessors. Like it or not, China must change its growth model. Until it does so it will be excessively vulnerable to changes in the trade surplus or in domestic investment.

So how will China adjust? Almost certainly it will adjust with much lower growth rates driven by a collapse in investment growth. Mahatma Gandhi famously complained that speed is irrelevant if you are going in the wrong direction, and clearly China is racing forward, but in the wrong direction. Until recently it was hard to find economists who expected annual Chinese GDP growth to drop much below 8–9 percent over the next decade, but the extent of the overinvestment problem has finally forced even the greatest optimists to reconsider.

As China fitfully tries to rebalance its economy, a small but rising number of Chinese economists are now beginning to predict sharply lower annual growth rates of 6 to 7 percent over the next few years. But the arithmetic of adjustment suggests growth is likely to be even lower, perhaps half that level.

How can China rebalance away from investment and toward domestic consumption as the main engine of growth? Only with great difficulty. Chinese households consume only about 34 percent of GDP, not much above half the global average and far less than the rate in any other country. It bears repeating that such a large domestic imbalance has no historical precedent.

Over the next ten years policymakers have said that they will try to raise consumption to 50 percent of GDP. Although this represents a substantial adjustment for China, it is worth remembering that 50 percent will still leave China with by far the lowest consumption rate of any major economy, and given the need for an equal and opposite adjustment by the low-savings economies of the rest of the world, it is not at all obvious that the world will be able to accommodate even this limited improvement in the imbalance in the Chinese economy. The world is desperate for demand, and foreigners may be unwilling to accommodate such a large gap between what China produces and what it consumes.

But even achieving this goal will be hard because it requires that household consumption grow 4 percentage points faster than GDP. To raise consumption from 34 percent of GDP to 50 percent of GDP in ten years, in other words, consumption growth must outpace GDP growth by 4 full percentage points every single year of the decade. If China's GDP grows at 10 percent annually for the next decade, for example, we would need consumption to grow by 14 percent annually in order to achieve the target.

Can China do it? In the past decade, Chinese household consumption has grown by 7 percent to 8 percent annually, while GDP has grown at an astonishing 10 percent to 11 percent. If one expects Chinese GDP to grow by 6 percent to 7 percent on average over the next decade, as increasingly pessimistic policymakers and advisors in Beijing are suggesting, Chinese household consumption would have to surge by 10 percent to 11 percent annually just to permit a rebalancing to 50 percent of GDP in ten years.

Such consumption growth is unlikely because powerful structural factors work against it. First and most obviously, the global environment is likely to be much less accommodating over the next decade than it was in the previous decade. Second, the Chinese growth model, remember, transfers income from households to the corporate and state sector, mainly in the form of artificially low interest rates, in order to generate such rapid growth. Low interest rates in particular sharply reduce borrowing costs for the state-owned companies that funnel this easy money into mega-investments.

The easy financing also gooses banks' profit margins and allows them to resolve bad loans with ease. If we see a surge in nonperforming loans, which almost everyone expects, low interest rates will be the prime mechanism for recapitalizing the banks and permitting insolvent borrowers to "grow" their way back into solvency.[11]

But of course this cheap borrowing will continue to come at the expense of household depositors. Low yields on deposits will force them to sacrifice consumption in order to raise savings to some target level. This will result in a continued downward pressure on consumption, making it hard for consumption growth in the next decade to outpace consumption growth in the past decade.

Can China Manage the Transition More Efficiently?

So what kind of GDP growth rates can we expect for China over the next decade? Even if consumption manages to keep growing at the same rate it has during the past decade, when Chinese and global conditions were buoyant and debt levels much lower, China's growth must slow to 3–4 percent at best to achieve real rebalancing. This is the impact, in other words, of the required reduction in investment, which will have to be sudden and sharp.

In a less optimistic scenario, consumption growth will slow down to less than what it was last decade— perhaps because of slower GDP growth— making rebalancing even harder. In that case for China to achieve real rebalancing, GDP growth rates will be even lower than 3 to 4 percent.

Will slower growth be a disaster for China, and will it lead to social instability? Not necessarily. If the rebalancing is well managed, by definition household income and consumption will grow faster than GDP, and so the lost decade of growth will not be as painful for the household sector as one might imagine. For example, one can easily posit a case in which China's GDP grows by 3 percent annually, Chinese household income grows at 5 percent, and consumption at 5 or 6 percent. In that case Chinese households will continue to feel better off and to have improving economic prospects.

But by definition if household income grows faster that GDP, there must implicitly be a transfer of resources from the state to the household sector. For much of the past three decade we have seen the opposite, so the household share of the rapidly growing pie has contracted while the state share has expanded. This must be reversed.

There is a "good" way to manage and speed up the process, and that is through some form of direct or indirect privatization of state assets. This would involve the government's recapitalizing the banks with state assets (because otherwise losses must be subsidized by households) and transferring resources from the state sector to the household sector in other ways. Remember that the key to raising the consumption share of GDP is to raise the household income share of GDP.

Transferring state assets to the private sector is, however, easier to say than to do, and there will be significant political constraints and resistance from vested interests that will make this transfer very difficult, as we saw at the beginning of this chapter. If Beijing is unable for domestic political or other reasons to accommodate direct transfers of state assets, with everything this must entail of corporate governance reform, there is a second, less "good" way for the transfer of state assets to the household and private sector, which is the way Japan stumbled upon after the 1990 crisis. This is simply to let the state continue absorbing private debt.

Government debt levels soaring faster than government assets, as they did in Japan after 1990, is effectively a transfer of wealth from the state sector to the private sector. In Japan after 1990 this allowed continued growth in Japanese household income and consumption (both of which sharply outpaced the less than 1 percent GDP growth Japan averaged after 1990).

State absorption of debt in China can have the same impact. This is a "less good" approach than the privatization approach because although it is politically much easier (no important sector or family actually has to give up control of state sector industries to be privatized), the problem with it, as Japan amply demonstrates, is that debt levels will soar and themselves become a huge constraint to future growth and reform.

Some More Misconceptions

The picture is not especially bright for GDP growth, but it is not especially gloomy for household income growth or social stability. China and the world should prepare for a world in which average Chinese GDP growth over the next decade is likely to be less than 3 or 4 percent annually—heavily frontloaded, with more now and less later. Along with it Chinese government debt will soar in much the same way government debt did in Japan after 1990.[12] Excluding a radical political transformation in which much of the state sector is turned over in a direct and meaningful way to the private sector, this is the only scenario under which China can meaningfully rebalance.

Before ending this chapter on China, I want to return to the article that I discussed at the end of chapter 3. In the article the author argued that the foreign exchange value of the renminbi does not matter to China's trade balance. This argument is widely made and widely believed (the author even calls them "home truths") but, as I hope to have demonstrated, wholly mistaken. The article made two other claims that are very common and also seriously mistaken. I show why they are mistaken in the next chapter as well as in chapters 6 and 7, but because they are so widespread—and seem at first glance to be very plausible—it is worth considering them.

> **American consumers have benefitted enormously from Chinese production efficiency.** While overall consumer prices in the U.S. have risen by 42 per cent over the last 15 years, prices of durable goods have fallen by 14 per cent. Average toy prices have come down 57 per cent. But have the people who made this possible ever received a word of thanks from the beneficiaries? Cup your hands to your ears. Listen hard.
>
> **Profligate American consumers who scorn savings rely on China to make the necessary investments in their country.** All the money that goes to China to pay for consumer rubbish flows right back in again as investment to make up for fiscal and trade deficits. This helps keeps interest rates down and the U.S. dollar strong.[13]

It is true of course that American consumers have benefitted from Chinese subsidies, but this is hardly a good thing in a country suffering from overconsumption. The reason no thanks have been offered is because this benefit comes with a cost. The dispute over trade is about employment and debt, not about each country helping the other consume, and to ignore them misses the point.

We explore why this is the case in chapters 5 and 7, but for the moment it is probably enough to point out that if China's subsidizing of American consumption is such an obviously good thing for Americans, it is puzzling why American attempts to reverse the process and subsidize Chinese consumption, by getting China to raise the value of the renminbi, are so strongly resisted by Beijing. After all, given the difference in wealth between Chinese and American consumers, it would be hard to argue that Americans deserve the favor more than the Chinese.

As for the second point—that the United States benefits not just from importing Chinese goods cheaply but also from importing Chinese savings—this is also wrong, and wrong in what should be a very obvious way. Exporting savings is not an act of generosity. To see why, please read on.

CHAPTER FIVE

The Other Side of the Imbalances

Because one country's trade surplus or deficit must be matched by an opposite deficit or surplus elsewhere, domestic policies, distortions, and institutional arrangements that affect the domestic trade balance must force obverse changes elsewhere. Specifically, any policy that affects the gap between savings and investment in one country must affect in an opposite way the gap between savings and investment in the rest of the world.

LET US LEAVE THE CHINESE REBALANCING and return to a more abstract discussion of trade imbalances. We are often told that countries that run large trade deficits do so because local households save too little. This, so the argument goes, is usually because of moral weaknesses or local cultural preferences that encourage lazy work habits and spendthrift ways, at either the private level or the public level, and often both.

The only thing that can correct a country's trade deficit, according to this view, is a return to old-fashioned virtues. If countries with large trade deficits only learned to save more and work harder the problem would be resolved. To put it a little differently, in a world where some countries save too much and others save too little, the best and really only solution is for the latter to increase their savings.

Can this possibly be true? Unfortunately, or perhaps fortunately, the reasoning behind these kinds of claims is nonsensical. In fact as I will show, although working harder (or, rather, more productively) might always boost economic growth, the proposed solutions of more thrift are likely to be bad both for global growth and for employment, and likely to make problems worse for both deficit and surplus countries.

Do countries that run large trade deficits suffer from households that save too little? By definition of course, a country running a trade deficit must have insufficient domestic savings compared to its domestic investment, but this doesn't mean it saves too little. It is nothing more than a tautology, and has no real meaning beyond the accounting identity.

More important, a country's savings rate is often not, as I have argued, simply a function of domestic savings culture or preferences. Very often it reflects the need for savings to balance at a global level, in which case foreign saving rates will affect domestic savings rates, and if high foreign savings are caused by foreign policy distortions, those same policy distortions can force low savings rates domestically.

We will see more explicitly how this can work in the example of Europe, which we will visit in chapter 6, but to begin the analysis it is important to remember that one of the accounting identities that I discussed in chapter 1, and an obvious one at that, is that the total of trade surpluses in the world must be exactly equal to the total of trade deficits in the world. To put it in another way, if one country's trade surplus rises, it must be counterbalanced either by an increase in another country's trade deficit or by a reduction in another country's trade surplus.

And because the trade balance for any country is equal to the gap between domestic savings and domestic investment, any change in the gap between investment and savings in one country must automatically be matched by an equal but opposite change in the gap between savings and investment elsewhere.[1] Together these two points suggest that it is a mistake to assume that savings in any country are simply a function of local preferences for thrift versus consumption. In fact policies in one country that affect the local gap between savings and investment, for example policies that force up the savings rate, can cause significant changes in the savings rate in another country.

How would this occur? No direction in the flow of causality is implied in the accounting identity, but assume that conditions in one country, Fredonia, change so that there is a rise in Fredonian consumption greater than the increase in total production of goods and services (i.e., total savings decline). Perhaps this happens because a surge in Fredonian real estate prices makes local households feel richer, and so leads them to increase their consumption out of current income. In this case, if Fredonia begins with perfectly balanced trade, the reduction in its savings relative to domestic investment will cause it to begin running a trade deficit.

Let me restate this to make it clear. In Fredonia we have assumed that savings and investment are exactly equal, in which case Fredonia neither imports nor exports capital on a net basis, and its current account balances to zero. We then assume that a surge in real estate prices makes Fredonians feel richer, and they increase their consumption out of current income. This causes their savings rate to drop, and unless there is an equivalent drop in investment (if anything, investment is likely to rise to take advantage of higher real estate prices) Fredonia must import foreign savings and so run a current account deficit.

There must of course be an equal and opposite reaction elsewhere. Because of the reduction in Fredonian savings, domestic interest rates will probably rise, and so Fredonia will end up attracting savings from abroad which, remember, on a net basis will be exactly equal to the new Fredonian trade or current account deficit.

There are only two ways that foreigners can accommodate the export of savings. Either investment abroad will decline, or savings abroad will rise (or some combination of both). Either of these can be a consequence of the increase in interest rates caused by the greater demand for foreign capital in Fredonian. That is, the higher cost of capital caused by Fredonian demand for foreign capital will reduce investment and credit-fueled consumption abroad and the higher return on capital will otherwise increase foreign savings.

The Fredonian real estate boom, in other words, will cause investment rates abroad to drop or savings to rise, or both, regardless of preferences abroad and even preferences in Fredonia. They are simply automatic consequences of the Fredonian real estate bubble. And just as the change in

Fredonia savings causes it to run a trade deficit, it also causes the rest of the world to run a trade surplus.

The causality can work in the other direction. Fredonia can put into place policies that force up the savings rate by repressing consumption, for example devaluing its currency or forcing down interest rates for businesses at the expense of savers or even, as Germany did in the 1990s, pushing through an agreement among labor, business, and the government to restrain wages. In this case Fredonia will run a trade surplus, and it will export abroad the foreign capital—and notice that because international capital flows are driven by excess savings in Fredonia rather than excess investment, they are likely to be accompanied by lower interest rates than in the previous case.

Once again Fredonian policies must be accompanied by equal and opposite changes abroad. Either foreign savings will decline (perhaps lower interest rates will encourage more foreign credit card consumer purchases) or foreign investment will rise as interest rates drop globally, or both.

Can Europe Change American Savings Rates?

The point is that in a globalized world in which trade and capital flow across national borders, consumption, production, savings, and investment in separate countries are all interconnected, and changes in one country must cause equivalent changes in another country. To move away from the abstract, imagine what would happen if European policymakers decided one day to subsidize the production of Airbus to such an extent that the cost of Airbuses dropped by 50 percent. Assume further that there was no U.S. retaliation. Would this affect the American savings rate?

At first glance many analysts and commentators would say that the answer should pretty obviously be no. If it were the spendthrift culture of Americans that caused low U.S. savings, it is hard to see why subsidizing the Airbus should have any impact on American savings rates at all. Why should European subsidies to airplane manufacturers change American cultural attitudes toward thrift?

But of course there is a lot more to it than culture. If Airbus were able to cut the price of its airplanes in half thanks to European government generosity, more airlines around the world would increase their purchases of Airbus planes in place of Boeing planes. With this tougher competition, Boeing would probably have to cut production down sharply and make and sell far fewer airplanes. It would close down factories and fire workers.

If the U.S. economy were growing quickly and unemployment were very low, the workers and assets released by Boeing would be diverted to produce other things, but the total value of these other things would have to be less than the total value of foregone Boeings, or else the workers would have been hired away anyway. On the other hand if the U.S. economy were growing slowly and unemployment were high, very few of the workers and resources devoted to building Boeing airplanes would be redeployed, and total U.S. production would drop even more.

At the same time the sharp reduction in the price of airplanes would almost certainly lower travel costs. This would boost consumption in the United States somewhat by increasing the purchasing power of American household income. Of course this would be counterbalanced by lower consumption caused by higher unemployment, but necessarily in the end total consumption in the United States would rise a little or at least would decline by less than total production.

Why? Because as long as less than 100 percent of the revenues generated by Boeing from selling airplanes goes to pay workers, or as long as workers save at least part of their wages, the total amount of lost consumption generated by lost Boeing sales must be less than the total amount of lost production generated by those lost sales. Add the fact that unemployed workers receive some form of worker compensation, or spend out of savings, and the net result of the Airbus subsidies will be a decline in U.S. production that substantially exceeds the decline in consumption.

But remember that everything that a country produces must be either consumed or saved. The only way for this accounting identity to balance is for American savings to have declined by the difference between the change in American consumption and the change in American production. And notice that as the American savings rate declined, unless there was an equal decline in the American investment rate the U.S. trade deficit must have immediately gone up.

So it turns out that a decision made in Brussels or Paris about subsidies to the Airbus caused both the American savings rate to decline and the American trade deficit to rise, in which case arguing that the United States is running a trade deficit "because" Americans save too little makes no sense at all except as a tautology. What happened in reality is that a policy decision made abroad, which affected the price of European airplanes, caused a change in the gap between total U.S. production and total U.S. consumption.

The changes in the American savings rate and in the trade deficit, in other words, were simply automatic consequences of the change in production relative to consumption. To counteract the impact of the Airbus subsidy, the U.S. government could have raised tariffs, subsidized Boeing by the same amount, or done a number of other things, but it would have had to intervene if it wanted to prevent the U.S. savings rate from falling. This fall in U.S. savings would have had nothing to do with changes in American cultural attitudes toward savings and consumption, and so could not be prevented except by government intervention.

But old habits die hard. The increase in the American trade deficit would almost certainly bring forth chest thumping about the decline of American virtue and exhortations from moralizing commentators that Americans become thriftier and work harder—perhaps becoming more like their European cousins, who, these same commentators will note, have just increased their savings rate and their trade surplus thanks to the sudden increase in their willingness to work harder and save more.[2]

But would the United States and the world really be better off if Americans took these exhortations to heart and increased their savings? Almost certainly not. A reduction in American consumption will not reduce the value of the Airbus subsidy, and so it will have little immediate impact on U.S. imports of Airbuses or, more important, on Boeing. It will, however, reduce demand for goods and services produced by both Americans and foreigners.

Depending on whether the economy is growing quickly or is stagnant, the reduction in demand could cause an increase in unemployment as American workers are fired in order to reduce the production of goods and services that are no longer purchased by Americans. Firing workers, of course, reduces household income and, with it, household consumption, and if the reduction in household consumption is greater than the reduction in the amount of goods and services produced domestically, the U.S. trade deficit certainly will decline.

But is this a good thing? It will require higher rates of unemployment both in the United States and abroad (after all, the reduction in American consumption will imply a reduction in American imports too).

How Does Trade Rebalance?

If the production of goods and services declines more slowly than consumption, perhaps because fired workers are entitled to unemployment benefits that allow them to maintain their lifestyles, U.S. savings will actually decline and the U.S. trade deficit might at first increase until brutal domestic prospects cause businesses to cut investment sharply. In that case the trade deficit will disappear, but only under conditions of very low savings, very low investment, and very high unemployment.

I am not suggesting that there is no value in thrift, but I do want to insist that in a globalized world it is not always obvious that the main cause of a country's domestic savings imbalances lies in domestic institutions or conditions. Any distortion in one country's position that affects its international trade and capital position must be reflected in an equal and opposite distortion elsewhere. The global balance of payments will always balance, one way or the other. Higher savings in one country must be met either with higher investment in that country or elsewhere, or with lower savings elsewhere. No other option is possible.

This, by the way, is at the heart of Ben Bernanke's global savings glut hypothesis. In a speech in early 2011 he asked,

Why was the United States, a mature economy, the recipient of net capital inflows that rose to as much as 6 percent of its gross domestic product prior to the financial crisis? A significant portion of these capital inflows reflected a broader phenomenon that, in the past, I have dubbed the global saving glut.

Over the past 15 years or so, for reasons on which I have elaborated in earlier remarks, many emerging market economies have run large, sustained current account surpluses and thus have become exporters of capital to the advanced economies, especially the United States. These inflows exacerbated the U.S. current account deficit and were also factors pushing U.S. and global longer-term interest rates below levels suggested by expected short-term rates and other macroeconomic fundamentals.[3]

One much-repeated criticism of Bernanke's global savings glut hypothesis was that whereas a global savings glut should imply a rise in global savings, in fact the total amount of savings in the world did not change much during the period of the glut. This objection, of course, fails to understand the functioning of the balance of payments. A global savings glut will not result in a sharp rise in global savings above the global investment level. It cannot.

It will be driven by a forced increase in savings in one part of the global economy, the source of the glut, that must be met, as a matter of arithmetical necessity, by an accommodating shift elsewhere. This shift will come as some combination of an increase in investment at home or abroad and a reduction in savings abroad. No other outcome is possible. Global savings gluts, in other words, do not necessarily or even often result in an increase in global savings. They more typically result in a shift in savings.

We return to this topic in chapters 6 and 7, when we look at a more specific case of how policy distortions can be transmitted from one country to another. As part of understanding how the global balance of payments mechanism works, however, it may first be useful to examine another widely held misconception about trade and trade adjustments.

In the debate about global trade imbalances, we often hear it said that because Americans produce nothing that China exports to the United States, any move to restrict Chinese imports to the United States would have no employment effect on Americans. A forced contraction in Chinese exports would simply result in an equivalent increase in the exports of some other country—let's call it Mexico. Mexico would benefit from U.S. trade action, but the United States wouldn't. This is a version of our discussion in chapter 2 about the Fredonian demand for widgets.

There are many reason for opposing trade restrictions and other forms of trade war between the two countries—the two most important being, in my opinion, first that trade war will result in slower global growth than a negotiated settlement, and second that the importance of the U.S.-China relationship involves a lot more than economic issues. A troubled relationship between the two countries spells potentially bad outcomes for issues such as the environment, global terrorism, and nuclear proliferation. But the argument that restrictions on Chinese trade will have no impact on U.S. employment is simply wrong and should not be part of the debate.

In the first place, China doesn't simply produce slippers, lighters, and toys to sell to the United States. Chinese growth is heavily capital intensive, far more than is appropriate for such a poor country (but not surprising given repressed interest rates), and China produces many things that Americans produce or used to produce until quite recently—including automobiles, steel, chemicals, advanced metal products, and, soon enough, aircraft. Remember also that China's import substitution policies will have as big an impact on trade as export support.

Anyway, it is hard to imagine that the explosion in U.S. imports from China in the past decade could consist of nothing that Americans produced themselves but were already importing from other countries. If that were truly the case, wouldn't China's rising exports and trade surplus in the past decade be balanced wholly by declining exports and trade surpluses in other countries? Total U.S. imports and the total American trade deficit should have held fairly steady. They didn't. The U.S. deficit rose in the decade before the crisis.

But even if we are wrong in assuming that there is any overlap in trade, and if the United States produces or can produce absolutely nothing that it purchases from China, it is irrelevant. The claim that there can be no employment impact in the United States of a contraction in Chinese trade could be conceivable only if all trade settled only on a bilateral basis.

Globalization Is Not Bilateral

There may have been a time, two or three hundred years ago, when trade settled mostly on a bilateral basis with exchanges of specie, but since the late nineteenth century, and certainly in the past few decades, trade has never settled bilaterally. It must settle multilaterally, in which case it is pointless to talk about the overlap between U.S. and Chinese production in determining how changes in one will affect changes in the other.

To see why, let us assume there are four countries in the world: China, the United States, Mexico, and Brazil. Let us also assume that because of significant export subsidies paid for by domestic consumers, China runs a large trade surplus with the United States whereas the other two countries have perfectly balanced accounts on both a bilateral and overall basis. Finally let us assume that China and the United States produce completely different sets of goods in which there is no overlap.

How would trade intervention work in that case? If the United States were to take actions to reduce Chinese exports to the United States by $100, perhaps by forcing an increase in the dollar value of the renminbi, Americans would still need to buy those goods from someone else, albeit at higher prices, since according to our admittedly unrealistic assumptions they do not and cannot produce them on their own.

Rather than buying these products from China, let us assume that Americans will buy them from Mexico. This means that nearly the full quantity of lost Chinese production would shift to Mexico (higher prices would reduce U.S. demand somewhat, but let us ignore that).

In that case it is pretty easy to imagine what would happen at first. Chinese workers would get fired as Chinese factories that sold to the United States closed, but on the other hand Mexicans would have to open new factories and hire workers to accommodate the $100 in increased exports. These new workers and factories would assume the full effort to produce the goods Americans consume. So not a single unemployed American would benefit, and American consumers would have to pay higher prices, while Mexicans get all the benefits of U.S. trade intervention against China, right?

Not quite. This isn't the end of the story. If Mexico does not intervene in its currency and banking system, two additional things are going to happen in Mexico. First, the peso will strengthen as demand for pesos rises among American importers. We can assume that the surge in exports causes no capital inflow into Mexico to take advantage of the better business prospects, but if it does, it would put even more upward pressure on the peso.

Of course a rising peso shifts income from Mexican exporters to Mexican households in the way we discussed in chapter 2. It also reduces the profitability and demand for other Mexican exports and so causes Mexican exporters to reduce other production by some amount. Total Mexican production in that case rises by less than $100, and either American or Brazilian production would increase to fill the gap.

Second, unemployed Mexican workers will now get jobs and will earn income that they weren't earning before. Real household income in Mexico will rise. Because it is a pretty safe bet that Mexican workers don't save 100 percent of their additional income, especially if they were formerly unemployed, Mexican consumption must also rise.

Notice, then, that total Mexican production rose by less than $100 and total Mexican consumption rose by some large amount, perhaps very close to $100. I am making the unreasonable assumption that there is no increase in Mexican investment associated with the increase in Mexican exports, but if there were any increase in investment, it would increase Mexico's domestic demand even further without initially increasing Mexican production.

So Mexico's trade surplus will not rise by anywhere near $100. It will rise by a lot less than that, and may even decline initially, depending on whether or not better business prospects cause an increase in domestic investment. Because the increase in the value of the renminbi shifted Mexican exports upward, this must mean that Mexican imports also increased, and if this is the case they must have imported from somewhere—perhaps from the United States or Brazil.

If the increase in Mexican imports were satisfied by increased U.S. exports, then of course there would likely be a positive impact on U.S. employment. Notice that what Mexico imports from the United States is of course not those goods that we have presumed that Americans cannot make. It imports from the United States a completely different set of goods—capital goods, creative goods, or anything else—but import it must.

If the Mexicans sourced part of this increase in imports from Brazil, then we have to go through the whole exercise for Brazil and come back to at least some additional U.S. exports to Brazil. *Mutatis mutandis* a reduction in China's trade surplus must result in a reduction in the U.S. trade deficit and an increase in U.S. employment as long as Brazil and Mexico don't themselves intervene in trade.

This is made evident by looking at capital flows. The reduction in Chinese exports to the United States must be matched by a reduction in capital that China exports to the United States. If total Chinese capital exports decline by $100 and total U.S. capital imports decline by $100, then by definition the Chinese trade surplus must have declined by that amount and the U.S. trade deficit must also have declined by the same amount. The fact that we ignorant mortals may not be able to predict or trace the exact way in which a forced renminbi revaluation will increase U.S. production and reduce the U.S. trade deficit is irrelevant. It will happen anyway.

One obvious flaw in this argument is that we have left China out of the rest of the process once we assumed the initial drop in its exports. But that isn't realistic—why couldn't the full increase in Mexico's imports come from a surge in Chinese exports to Mexico?

In fact it could, if China intervened to counter the impact of declining exports to the United States, say by reducing interest rates or by increasing subsidies to manufacturers in other ways. The rebalancing impact of an increase in the value of the renminbi would be offset by higher subsidies, paid for of course by the Chinese household sector. In that case China's trade surplus could even rise.

This would ultimately create a worse problem for both China and the world, especially for Mexico, who will be dragged even deeper into the unsustainable U.S.-China imbalances. It would mean that China still imported demand from a world struggling with low growth while, at the same time, worsening its domestic imbalances, perhaps by increasing investment in a country where investment levels are already dangerously high. And it would mean that U.S. unemployment remained where it was.

So what can we conclude from this little exercise? Three things. First, the no-overlap argument—that the United States cannot benefit from a reduction in the Chinese trade surplus because the United States produces nothing that China sells—is silly. Not only does the United States produce (or could produce) many things that China sells, but more important it doesn't matter whether or not it does. Trade does not have to settle bilaterally. In fact it almost never does.

Second, what matters is the totality of Chinese intervention. If a rising renminbi or trade tariffs in the United States are met by countermeasures within China, there might very well be no net trade rebalancing and even more dangerous distortions within the Chinese economy. That is why it is probably better for policymakers to target trade surpluses rather than just the currency, or just interest rates, or just wages, or just taxes, or just direct subsidies, or just any of a dozen factors.

The third conclusion is that all these things matter in the United States too. Measures targeted just at China might or might not work, depending on the Chinese response, and the wrong Chinese response can make both countries worse off (much worse off in the case of China). If the United States really wants to see its trade deficit decline, it should move aggressively to alter the balance between domestic production and consumption in a more permanent way—perhaps by raising consumption taxes, although this will work mainly by increasing U.S. and Chinese unemployment if China increases its intervention in the currency or in interest rates and credit. In that case we would be in a beggar-thy-neighbor world, and in that world global unemployment always rises.

The Global Shopping Spree

Before closing this chapter it is worth identifying and discussing one of the occasionally popular strategies proposed by policymakers as an effective way to close trade gaps. By evaluating the strategy in terms of its impact on savings and capital flows, we can see whether in fact this strategy can work and, if so, how it works.

The strategy involves national shopping expeditions, in which the leaders of a country with an excessively high trade surplus visit a major deficit country, usually the United States, and announce huge purchases, usually of expensive capital goods. In the 1980s, when Japan's very large trade surplus was a source of global trade tension, this was one of the favored policies of the Japanese government, who would embark on occasional shopping sprees during which government and corporate officials would visit the United States or Europe and announce a huge purchase of goods—often consisting of airplanes, high-tech equipment, capital goods, and so on.

These shopping sprees were politically very popular, and it is easy to see why. They provided widely broadcast media sessions, with beaming executives from Japan and the recipient country announcing large trade deals. Politicians in the recipient country could count the revenues from the various deals, impute from the deals the number of jobs created or saved, and announce a great success with very specific employment generation.

And yet, for all the shopping, the Japanese trade surplus never seemed to decline until after Japan began its great rebalancing in 1990, when the trade surplus managed a steep decline as a share of global GDP even without being aided by Japanese shopping sprees. In spite of its limited success in the Japan case, however, policymakers in both surplus and deficit countries still seem to love the strategy. In May 2012 a senior trade official from the United States proposed the same idea to me, but this time with China replacing

Japan as the prime shopper. Why couldn't China head off American criticism of its trade policies, he asked, by engaging in a similar shopping spree?

If, for example, China were to divert its purchases of Airbuses, to take a controversial example, and buy only Boeings, it would presumably cause a sharp reduction in the U.S. trade deficit by increasing Boeing exports. Europe of course wouldn't be happy, but because trade tensions with the United States were much more serious and important for China, and because Europe was in too weak of a position to complain, this might nonetheless be a very useful strategy for both China and the United States to follow.

It turns out, however, that as intuitively appealing it might seem to assume that increased government-sponsored purchases by China of American goods would reduce the U.S. trade deficit, in fact the truth is a lot more complex. Such a plan might have no impact on the overall American and European trade balances, although it would have a significant impact on the relative composition of the exports and imports of each country.

To see why, let us assume that China suddenly and unexpectedly announces that it will buy $10 billion of Boeings this year. There are two ways in which it can do this. It can buy new Boeings without changing any other behavior, in which case it will still buy just as many Airbuses and Boeings as it had planned to buy before the announcement, with an additional $10 billion in new planes beyond its original needs.

What will it do with these planes? Clearly it must use them for something beyond its normal transportation requirements since the existing purchase plan, before the special announcement, should in principle already satisfy Chinese needs. The new purchase would be in addition to its already planned purchases. Perhaps China could mothball these new planes, or turn them into amusement parks, or melt them down for the metal and scrap.

China would directly or indirectly finance these purchases by exchanging $10 billion of U.S. Treasury bonds for $10 billion of Boeing airplanes. What would the global trade impact be in that case? The answer is pretty straightforward. Chinese current account imports from the United States would increase by $10 billion, and Chinese capital account exports to the United States would decline by the same amount, as the country sold off a portion of the U.S. Treasury bonds held by the central bank.

Nothing else would change in the global balance of payments. The Chinese trade surplus, in that case, would decline by $10 billion and the U.S. trade deficit would also decline by $10 billion. American unemployment would decline. Europe would be wholly unaffected.

Of course this is not a realistic case because it requires an additional purchase of goods that China doesn't need, and it is unlikely that China would purchase $10 billion of new Boeings just to turn them into amusement parks. It is true that Chinese policymakers are able to do things that policymakers in more transparent and accountable systems with firm budget constraints cannot do, but an unnecessary purchase of that magnitude in such a poor country would nonetheless create problems.

Trade Remains Unbalanced

Far more likely when China unexpectedly announces the $10 billion order is that it uses this purchase to fill existing demand. In that case China would simply divert $10 billion of orders it would have given to other producers of airplanes—let us call them all Airbus—over this and the next few years, in other words, and give them to Boeing. Chinese demand for airplanes would remain constant over the near term, but the Boeing share of that demand would grow by $10 billion at the expense of Airbus.

Would the United States in this case benefit from lower unemployment and Europe lose out with higher unemployment? This strategy might not be good for the world, and certainly not good for Europe, but it seems that it would be good for the United States and, because it reduces American anger at Chinese trade practices, it would be good for China too.

It turns out, however, that this simple and intuitive understanding of the trade impact of China's decision is wrong. If we focus on how this $10 billion order affects global capital flows and, through them, the overall trade balance, it becomes a lot less obvious that the United States benefits and Europe suffers.

The first point to consider is that if China spends $10 billion less in Europe buying Airbuses and $10 billion more in the United States buying Boeings, the net impact on China's current account is zero. Its current account surplus, in other words, will not change. This means that China's capital account deficit will also remain unchanged—China will export as much capital before it makes the decision as it will after it makes the decision, and it will export a net amount exactly equal to the current account surplus.

But the same is true for the United States and Europe. Their overall trade balances are going to be determined by their net capital positions, and if China exports the same amount of capital to the United States as it would have had it not made the decision to buy Boeings, which is the most likely scenario, the United States will have to run exactly the same current account deficit it was anyway going to run. In other words the Chinese purchase of Boeings will cause either an equivalent increase in American imports or an equivalent reduction in other American exports—or some combination of the two—so that the net impact on the American trade deficit is zero.

How the United States adjusts depends on a variety of factors, but it will occur through the impact of the Boeing purchases on American wages, American interest rates, and the value of the U.S. dollar in the foreign exchange markets. As these things all rise, they will make other American goods less competitive in foreign markets and foreign goods more competitive in the American market. The result for the United States and the world can be net positive or net negative, but it is not obvious just from the fact of the purchase which it will be.

We can pursue the analysis further. If the United States is in a recession, with high unemployment and weak investment demand, the increased purchases of Boeings by China will have a limited impact on wages and the cost of capital. Instead Boeing will hire unemployed workers, and total American consumption will rise because unemployed workers will have jobs. In that case the United States will export more (the Boeings) and will also import more by the same amount, so that while the American current account deficit does not change, the American economy will grow and unemployment will decline.

Of course if Europe is also in a recession, with high unemployment and weak investment demand, the opposite will occur. Its current account deficit will not grow, but the reduction in European exports (fewer Airbuses sold) will largely be matched by a reduction in European imports caused by rising domestic unemployment.

If, on the other hand, the United States and Europe are in good economic shape, with low unemployment and reasonably strong investment demand, the Chinese shopping spree once again will have no impact on their current account balances, but the increase in American airplane exports will be largely matched by a reduction in other exports, and the decline in European airplane exports will be largely matched by an increase in other exports.

This doesn't necessarily mean that there is no net economic impact in either country. By reducing other American exports and increasing Boeing exports, the shopping spree can be seen as a kind of industrial policy that diverts resources from the economy in general to Boeing in particular. If productivity growth in Boeing is expected to be higher than in other industries, or if there are greater positive externalities associated with airplane manufacturing, the diversion will be positive for the United States. If the opposite is true, it will be negative. The converse, of course, is true for Europe.

National shopping sprees, in other words, have little to no net impact on the overall balance of trade because they do not affect net capital flows. Strict market economists would argue that they are probably wealth destroying in the aggregate because a political decision to buy products from one country and not another is usually economically less efficient than a nonpolitical decision.

There are nonetheless clearly winners and losers. In this case Boeing will be a winner, but its gains could easily come at the expense of the rest of the American economy. Airbus will lose, but for the same reason its losses might be paid for by gains for other European businesses. One thing however is certain. National shopping sprees are likely to have little to no impact on a country's trade surplus or trade deficit, and whether or not they benefit the recipient country depends on a wide range of factors.

The analysis of the net benefits of national shopping sprees, it turns out, is not nearly as simple as we often assume. Of course when we can clearly identify the winners of a policy but the losers are hard to identify, the policy becomes politically a very attractive one. Boeing, in other words will always be happy with a shopping spree that involves Boeings. Other companies in the United States may or may not agree, but they will be hard to identify.

For this reason alone we should expect national shopping sprees to continue, even though rather than shopping sprees a far more effective policy would be reverse investment sprees. If China, for example, rather than buying $10 billion of Boeings, simply agreed to buy $10 billion less of U.S. dollar assets (say U.S. government bonds) and replace them with $10 billion more of European assets, the American trade deficit and the European trade surplus would decline by exactly that amount—less of course any subsequent shift in capital flows from Europe to the United States caused by the resulting strengthening of the euro. But it is hard for politicians to claim credit for a reduction of foreign buying of U.S. government bonds, even though, as we demonstrate in chapter 8, this would leave the United States better off.

CHAPTER SIX

The Case of Europe

The European crisis is a crisis of relative competitiveness within Europe, and the balance sheet crises are simply a consequence of domestic trade imbalances. The only three possible resolutions are (1) a reversal of the trade imbalances, which requires that Germany stimulate demand to the extent that it runs a large trade deficit, (2) many years of high unemployment, including, soon enough, in Germany, or (3) the breakup of the euro and sovereign debt restructuring for much of peripheral Europe including, possibly, France.

IN CHAPTER 5 I ARGUED THAT policy or institutional distortions in one country that affected its savings rates would also affect savings, but in the opposite way, in other countries. This is a very important point, and it is worth repeating. To say that a country runs a trade deficit because its citizens are spendthrift and save too little is meaningless—although perhaps permitting a frisson of moral smugness—and indicates only how little many analysts understand the global balance of payments mechanism.

One of the clearest ways to see how distortions in consumption in one country can cause distorted savings in another is by examining Europe since the creation of the euro. Because all of the eurozone countries have to share currency and monetary policies under the euro, the workings of their various trade imbalances become especially clear. This is perhaps most obvious when we examine Spain, a country that, before the crisis, had, unlike Germany, low government debt and fiscal surpluses and did not seem to be a model of spendthrift laziness.

Membership in the euro area was seen in Spain as a tremendous policy success for many years, and as a vindication of Spain's return to the civilized fold after many years of dictatorship under General Francisco Franco, but the European crisis has seriously tarnished that experience. On November 20, 2011, Spanish voters voted overwhelmingly to throw out the ruling Socialist Party, which was widely seen as having mismanaged the financial crisis from which Spain had been suffering in the previous two years. A desperate country reeling from high levels of unemployment was eager for a new government and a new set of leaders to fix Spain's economy.

But while José Luis Rodríguez Zapatero, the outgoing Socialist prime minister, can certainly be accused of having mismanaged the Spanish economy—as someone far more committed to fashionable but empty gestures than to accomplishment—it is unfair to blame the depth of the crisis on his policies. In fact I suspect that within a year the Partido Popular, the party that trounced the Socialists in 2011, will be as unpopular and as despised as were the Socialists.

Why? Because for all his inability to lead, former prime minister Zapatero really had only two unpalatable choices facing him. Either Spain must accept stagnant economic growth and unemployment levels of 20 percent or more for many years, or it must leave the euro. Because he refused the second and so had to suffer the first, the popularity of his party took a vicious beating.

Unfortunately the current prime minister, Mariano Rajoy, has exactly the same two options. He will be forced into accepting something that is either unpalatable to the political elite of both parties, abandoning the euro, or unpalatable to the electorate, accepting low or negative growth and extremely high levels of unemployment for many, many years.

Spanish costs and wages have been uncompetitive for nearly a decade, and the only way the country was able to grow for many years prior to the crisis was with a surge in domestic credit that expanded the nontradable goods sector—real estate and consumption, for the most part, with surging real estate itself fueling further borrowing and consumption. But of course since the 2007–8 crisis, Spain has no longer been able to keep domestic credit growing, and real estate prices have been falling rapidly.

So now Spain has no choice but to adjust domestic costs and wages downward. There are two ways it can do so. The first way is to force workers to accept high levels of unemployment for many years, as wages are ground down. The second way is for Spain to leave the euro and devalue its currency. Unfortunately these are likely to be the only two options for Madrid.

There is in fact an alternative solution, but it seems unlikely to be implemented without a radical change in German understanding and commitment to Europe. If Germany were to stimulate domestic consumption massively by reducing income and VAT taxes, turning its trade surplus into an equally large deficit, Spain and the other deficit countries of Europe would be able to grow their way back into health and earn the euros to repay their external debt. But if Germany continues to insist on keeping its trade surplus from contracting sufficiently, and all the evidence suggests that Germany will insist, there is simply no way Spain can grow and repay the debt.

Madrid can speak excitedly about reforming labor laws and improving business efficiency as a way of lowering Spain's cost basis, but although these reforms may have some positive effect, they will never be enough to make a difference. The fundamental problem has as much to do with external distortions that led to trade imbalances as with domestic. The numbers tell how divergent costs have become. According to data from the European Central Bank, unit labor costs in Spain rose 30 percent or more in the past decade, and even more in countries like Ireland, Greece, Italy, and Portugal. In Germany they rose only 5 percent.

In that case, without abandoning the euro Madrid can make Spain competitive only through a long period of high unemployment and sharply lower wages. As long as Germany remains intransigent and refuses to inflate domestic consumption, the Partido Popular will face the same choice the Socialists had: leave the euro or accept very high unemployment for many years.

Spain is already past the point at which it can recover on its own. In fact I believe it is moving inexorably toward crisis. This is simply part of the logic of what economists call "financial distress," and there is nothing mysterious about this process.

The Mechanics of Crisis

Why must Spain suffer an economic crisis? It is widely understood in economic theory that financial distress costs for overly indebted businesses are actually incurred not at bankruptcy but long before, when weakening credit forces stakeholders to behave in ways that undermine growth and reinforce credit deterioration. This explains why crises tend to move slowly at first and then suddenly spin out of control in a way that is almost impossible to halt without a major external intervention.

The same thing happens to overly indebted countries. When do countries have too much debt? The short answer is that they have too much debt when the market believes they have too much debt. This may seem a trite and even meaningless answer, but in fact understanding it is key to understanding the process of financial collapse.

When the market and other economic agents believe that a sovereign borrower has too much debt, they create a series of events that exacerbate the debt problem. The process works in a straightforward way. As the fiscal credibility of the government declines, it automatically forces nearly all the major sectors of the economy to change their behavior in reaction to this decline, and these changes in behavior force further decline. The process is slow at first, but because it is self-reinforcing, like all self-reinforcing processes it can reach a point beyond which it suddenly accelerates and spins out of control.

1. The most obvious way in which this change in behavior happens is in the behavior of creditors and investors. When doubts are raised about the solvency of the government, creditors naturally and automatically raise lending rates and shorten maturities. This raises default probabilities by increasing the cost of servicing the debt and, more important, by making the balance sheet ever more fragile. Shorter maturities, or insistence on seniority, increase the fragility of balance sheets by making them more vulnerable to adverse shocks. Of course this increased fragility itself increases the probability of default.

The government will excoriate these creditors and investors as speculators intent on harming the country, but while there may be some truth in the accusation, the anger misses the point. In fact all creditors, even official creditors, behave more or less in the same way—simply note the unseemly fight among official creditors during the Greek restructuring in early 2012, each of which demanded seniority and tried to exempt itself from accepting a write-down.[1]

2. But unfortunately it doesn't stop with just the behavior of creditors and speculators. Ordinary households, for example, also must react. They know that throughout history fiscal crises have usually been resolved by eroding the value of savings through inflation or depreciation. The threat that the government will freeze bank deposits and devalue the currency causes them to cash in their deposits and take the money out of the country. This reduces lending sharply and slows growth, while eliminating what is normally a very stable funding base.

3. What's more, because governments have taxing authority, and because businesses are easy political targets in a crisis, declining government credibility automatically changes private business behavior too. Instead of funding the investment that will generate future economic activity—especially given weaker growth prospects and higher interest rates—factories and shops close down, businesses disinvest, and entrepreneurs leave the country. As they do, workers lose jobs, growth is reduced further, and so debt-servicing capacity drops.

4. Workers, too, must respond to the crisis. As unemployment rises unions get more radical and labor agitation increases. Workers who are able to obtain protection have a kind of seniority that forces even more of the difficulty on workers who aren't able to lock in protection—it is interesting to note that during the Great Depression, for example, Americans with jobs saw their real income grow substantially even as unemployment soared. As unions and workers agitate and fight, it further weakens growth prospects for the country by raising both business and political uncertainty.

5. Finally—and the historical precedents are very clear here—policymakers themselves respond in ways that reinforce the crisis. As political instability rises and extremist parties become more powerful, politicians respond by promoting self-serving policies aimed at staying in power and that primarily address short-term problems even if these hurt longer-term growth prospects. As domestic politics become more unstable and localized, international cooperation declines. In her book on the politics of adjustment in the 1930s, Beth Simmons pointed out,

> A profile emerges of the domestic political characteristics associated with benign, norm-abiding adjustment during the interwar years: stable governments and quiescent labor movements contributed to international economic cooperation, while domestic political and social instability undermined it.[2]

More telling, in the context of Greece and, soon, other European countries, she underlined the relationship between declining credibility and international assistance:

> One of the primary reasons the French were denied financial assistance between 1925 and 1929 was that there was little confidence that the unstable Cartel de Gauches would implement a financial and fiscal policy that would prevent the hemorrhage of private capital from France. One of the most significant reasons for the breakdown of international cooperation as the British struggled to maintain sterling's parity in 1931 was that foreign central bankers were demanding bigger unemployment compensation cuts than the Labour Party could supply.[3]

As European officials make demands on Greece, and on other afflicted countries, that are politically unacceptable domestically, those involved are condemned to follow the same brutal road of collapsing cooperation. The political process, unfortunately, is self-reinforcing.

These predictably adverse changes in the behavior of at least five major groups of stakeholders are already happening in Spain and much of Europe. A rising probability of default, in other words, has forced most of the major sectors of the economy into behavior that is causing balance sheets systematically to weaken and economic growth prospects systematically to decline. More and riskier debt and slower growth, of course, increase the probability of default further, and so these sectors are forced even more urgently into accelerating their behavior.

Too Late

It is very hard to stop the process once it begins, and it is probably already too late for Spain and much of peripheral Europe, but while Europe stumbles toward debt crisis, Spain is trying hard to distance itself from countries like Greece, Portugal, and Italy. Madrid hopes investors will make a permanent distinction between responsible Spain and the less responsible countries that will be forced into abandoning the euro. It wants to be seen, in other words, as one of the virtuous countries that work hard, save, and repay their debts, and not one of the vicious ones.

But this strategy is the wrong one. Spain and the rest of peripheral Europe are suffering from the same set of problems, and these often enough have very little to do with virtue or vice (although clearly there is plenty of policy mismanagement).

These problems are often the consequences of many years of bad policy, driven just as much by bad German policies as by bad policies at home. If this is indeed the case, the problems of Spain and peripheral Europe can best be addressed only with a German adjustment at least as serious as the adjustment in peripheral Europe. Germany must stimulate domestic consumption and reverse its trade surplus, as difficult as this will be.

But Germany refuses to do so, implicitly insisting that most of peripheral Europe's problems were caused by misguided policies in those countries, and so also insisting that all the adjustments be made by Spain and peripheral

Europe. Germany is effectively taking the same position lampooned by Franklin Delano Roosevelt in 1932 as the Republican position:

A puzzled, somewhat skeptical Alice asked the Republican leadership some simple questions:

"Will not the printing and selling of more stocks and bonds, the building of new plants and the increase of efficiency produce more goods than we can buy?"

"No," shouted Humpty Dumpty, "the more we produce the more we can buy."

"What if we produce a surplus?"

"Oh, we can sell it to foreign consumers."

"How can the foreigners pay for it?"

"Why, we will lend them the money."

"I see," said little Alice, "they will buy our surplus with our money. Of course these foreigners will pay us back by selling us their goods."

"Oh not at all, "said Humpty Dumpty. "We set up a high wall called the tariff."

"And," said Alice at last, "how will the foreigners pay off these loans?"

"That is easy, said Humpty Dumpty. "Did you ever hear of a moratorium?"

And so alas, my friends, we have reached the heart of the magic formula of 1928.[4]

This won't work, except at a tremendous cost. The only solution that can minimize the pain for Spain and the rest of Europe requires that the countries that have suffered most from the unbalanced growth of the past decade band together and force all of Europe, including Germany, to make the necessary adjustments. By threatening to leave the euro together unless Germany adjusts, they will effectively force Germany to adjust anyway. Their abandonment of the euro and devaluation will push up the value of the euro sharply and cause a collapse in the German export machine, but this adjustment will be much more disorderly.

In order to understand why, it is important to understand what caused the crisis and Germany's role in it. Confused moralizers love to praise high-savings countries (let us call them all "Germany") for their hard work and thrift, and deride high-consuming countries (which we will call "Spain") as lazy and too eager to spend more than they earn. The world cannot possibly rebalance, they argue, until the latter become more like the former.

This is almost wholly nonsensical. As I have tried to show in this book, culture and individual preferences may cause some of us to save more of our income and others to save less, but when entire countries have persistent abnormally high or low savings rates, individual preferences are almost never the reason. Abnormal savings rates over long periods of time are largely consequences of trade and industrial policies at home and abroad that have distorted the relationship between domestic production and sustainable domestic consumption.

In fact, domestic policies by the German government can explain not only high German savings but also high Spanish consumption before the 2007–8 crisis and high Spanish unemployment since then. Both of these conditions were caused by the same set of European trade and capital imbalances driven largely by distortions in German policies.

After German reunification in the early 1990s, Germany faced the problem of very high domestic unemployment. It resolved this by putting into place a number of policies, agreed on by trade unions, businesses, and the government, aimed at constraining wages and consumption and expanding production in order to regain competitiveness and generate jobs. Although these policies may have made sense for Germany and the world in the 1990s, a time during which Germany did not run the enormous trade surpluses it ran in the following decade (in fact it often ran very large trade deficits), the creation of the euro introduced a new set of currency and monetary rigidities that would change the impact of these policies both within Germany and abroad.

Specifically, as wage growth was constrained in Germany by relatively tight monetary policy in the German context, it was left unconstrained in peripheral Europe because monetary policy there was, paradoxically, too loose given underlying conditions of rapid growth and rising prices. These policies resulted in an increasingly undervalued euro for Germany relative to the rest of Europe, low wages for its level of productivity, high consumption and income taxes, and expensive infrastructure funded by these taxes.

In that case it is not surprising that German GDP growth exceeded the growth in German household income, because households were effectively forced to subsidize employment growth, and this subsidy reduced disposable household income and consumption relative to total production. But these policies should not have remained in place for as long as they did because although they allowed Germany to grow faster than it otherwise would have, thanks to the relative increase in German competitiveness, they would necessarily create economic distortions at the expense of the rest of Europe.

How so? With German GDP growth exceeding consumption growth for many years, by definition the German savings rate had to rise. National savings, after all, are simply national production less national consumption.

German Thrift

The high German savings rate, in other words, had very little to do with whether Germans were ethnically or culturally programmed to save—contrary to the prevailing cultural stereotype. It was largely the consequence of policies aimed at generating rapid employment growth by restraining German consumption in order to subsidize German manufacturing—usually at the expense of manufacturers elsewhere in Europe and the world.

One of the automatic consequences of these policies was that Germany began running large trade surpluses to generate domestic growth and higher employment. What did this have to do with Spain? It turns out that Spain's low savings rate was itself a consequence of the combination of Germany's high savings rate and monetary union. It was not primarily the consequence of Spanish policies, nor even the consequence of Spain's famously relaxed Mediterranean culture.

Why? Because those large German surpluses had to result in trade deficits elsewhere. Thanks to Europe's monetary policies driven by the needs of Germany—a strong euro and low interest rates—the deficits showed up primarily in peripheral Europe. Before the creation of the euro, Italy, Spain, France, Greece, and Portugal had occasionally run fairly large trade deficits—in total they show up among the top ten deficit countries fourteen times during the decade of the 1990s, although it is worth noting that they also appear among the top ten trade surplus countries fourteen times during the same pre-euro decade.

Only after monetary union did their trade deficits explode. In the decade after 2000 those same countries show up forty-two times among the top ten deficit nations and never among the surplus countries. This cannot have been a coincidence. The most obvious reason for this is the currency. If Germany's currency is undervalued relative to its European partners, by definition Spain's must be overvalued, and not surprisingly, Germans will tend to underconsume relative to production and Spaniards to overconsume. These are always fairly standard consequences of overvalued and undervalued exchange rates, for the reasons discussed in chapter 2 and chapter 3.

But there is more. If German anticonsumption policies force up the German savings rates and the German trade surplus, and European monetary policies force those surpluses onto the rest of Europe, there are only four options from which Spain (and the rest of peripheral Europe) can choose:

1. The increase in the gap between German savings and investment must be matched by an opposite shift in the gap elsewhere. One way for this to happen is if the Spanish investment rate can rise above the savings rate enough to push Spain into a trade deficit large enough to match Germany's surplus. Because German policies are likely to erode the profitability of Spanish manufacturing, private investment in the tradable goods sector is unlikely to rise, but investment in

infrastructure can, funded by German capital. This means, of course, that Spanish debt must rise.

Alternatively German capital exports to Spain at very low interest rates relative to the change in Spanish prices (Spain, in other words, suffered from low or even negative real interest rates) can fund a real estate boom that forces up Spanish investment sufficiently to absorb the increase in German savings exported abroad. If Spain lacks sufficient housing, this is a good thing. The risk of course is that if it continues long enough it can fund a real estate bubble.

2. Another way for the gap between Spanish savings and investment to accommodate the increase excess of German savings over investment is for Spanish savings to drop. Spain can allow domestic consumption, for example, to rise faster than GDP, which by definition means a declining savings rate and a rising trade deficit. This is usually caused by rising consumer financing funded, again, by German capital exports at low or negative real interest rates, or as CUNY professor David Harvey put it, "The gap between what labour was earning and what it could spend was covered by the rise of the credit card industry and increasing indebtedness."[5] This was especially likely since the European Central Bank kept interest rates artificially low to suit German needs—where prices and wages were rising much more slowly than in Spain.

3. Spain could also have refused to absorb excess German savings. For example, it could have cut fiscal spending and raised taxes enough to cause domestic unemployment to rise. Raising interest rates sharply of course was not an option because as a member of the eurozone Spain could not control rates. Ironically this option was impossible to implement except when the inevitable debt crisis forced up Spanish rates.

High unemployment would have brought down the Spanish savings rate by causing production to fall faster than consumption, although because investment would have probably declined under these conditions (why invest in new production when people don't have money to spend?), unemployment would have had to rise substantially unless these policies were combined by an increase in Spanish government borrowing and infrastructure investment.

4.   Spain could also in principle have refused to absorb excess German savings by lowering effective labor costs or by devaluing its currency against Germany's currency or could have imposed trade barriers. This would have effectively forced German savings back onto Germany. If it were possible to lower labor costs sufficiently, not just by reducing wages but by otherwise reducing the costs for business, this would have been the "best" way to do so, but it is unlikely that the cost of business, which is certainly higher in Spain than is optimal, could be lowered sufficiently to make up the difference.

In either of these two latter cases (options 3 or 4) Germany must adjust, either with a rise in domestic unemployment or with an increase in state investment. Of course under conditions of membership in the eurozone, Spain was not able to exercise either of these options.

Forcing Germany to Adjust

So Spain would have had to respond to German policies in a limited number of ways. It could have increased domestic investment, most easily in the form of a real estate bubble. It could have allowed consumption to surge and so savings to drop. It could have allowed unemployment to rise. Or it could have intervened in trade.

None of these were likely to be attractive response for Spain, but notice that these four options are automatic consequences of policies that affect the differential growth rates between German GDP and German consumption and were not caused by Spanish policies. Spain could have chosen only some combination among these four, and one way or the other it was forced to accept the undesired consequences of domestic German policies.

Before the 2007–8 crisis, as interest rates were kept too low, Spain more or less automatically accepted the first and second options (with investment going mostly into excess real estate). In other words Spain experienced both a boom in real estate construction, a boom so dramatic that it led to a vast oversupply of residential real estate through the country, and a consumption boom that drove down the domestic savings rate. This may not have been what it wanted, but if it was going to absorb the growth in German savings relative to German investment, it could do so only by having Spanish investment grow relative to Spanish savings.

Now that debt levels have risen so high in Spain that the government's credit has been impaired and Spanish interest rates have soared, both the Spanish real estate boom and the boom in Spanish consumption are collapsing. But as long as Germany's policies have not been reversed, Spain is still forced to choose among the four options.

It has, of course, reluctantly accepted the third. Unemployment in Spain has soared as the Spanish economy tries to adjust by rejecting the import of excess German savings. Unless Germany reverses the policies that create these excess savings, Spain will continue to suffer from very high unemployment either until after many, many years domestic wages have adjusted sufficiently, or until it chooses to the fourth option and intervenes in trade. Both of these will be painful for Germany because they effectively force German savings back home, and Germany will have to choose between either a surge in domestic investment or a drop in domestic savings—most easily accomplished by a surge in unemployment—in order to rebalance.

These four options available to Spain, it must be stressed again, are the automatic consequence of German policy, and as long German policy distortions persist, they are the only options open to Spain. Spanish policy mismanagement may have made things worse, but even the best government would have been forced to choose among these four largely unwelcome policies.

This is the key point: no matter what reforms Prime Minister Rajoy implements over the next year or two, as long as German distortions persist Spain can choose only among these four options, and because the first two require a sharp increase in debt, which is probably no longer possible, the only options realistically remaining for Spain are the last two: either it must accept high unemployment for many years or it must intervene in trade, most easily by abandoning the euro and allowing its new currency to depreciate against the euro.

For this reason the solutions to the European imbalances don't need exhortations that Spaniards become as virtuous, thrifty, and hardworking as Germans. Virtue has nothing to do with it, and in the face of rising unemployment it is meaningless to ask Spaniards to work more, nor can Spain escape from the mess by convincing its population to spend less.

Two-Sided Adjustment

On the contrary, reduced Spanish consumption will simply cause Spanish (and German) unemployment to rise even further. The optimal solution instead requires a combination of policies that simultaneously force faster GDP growth relative to household income growth in Spain and faster household income growth in Germany. Without a change in German policies, there is little Spain can do to improve matters. It is impossible to expect Spain to repay its debt to Germany, in other words, unless Germany runs a trade deficit and Spain a trade surplus. This is just the constraint posed by the accounting identity, and it cannot possibly be violated (except by forcing a huge European current account surplus onto the rest of the world, which does not resolve the problem so much as force it onto non-Europeans).

Spain and the peripheral countries of Europe are in trouble, for faults of their own, of course, but the analysis is incomplete until we recognize that they are in trouble also because of German policies aimed at generating rapid employment growth at the expense of its European partners. Their problems cannot be resolved in an optimal way unless Germany reverses these policies. For this reason the deficit countries must band together and force a sharing of the adjustment cost across Europe.

If only Spain and the peripheral countries are forced to adjust, they can do so through economic stagnation and many years of high unemployment. But the threat that they will take steps together to force unemployment back onto Germany, perhaps by abandoning the euro together, is the one way that German policymakers can be convinced to stop criticizing lazy southerners and take concrete steps to rebalance their own distorted economy.

More than seventy years ago John Maynard Keynes explained that trade imbalances are caused by misguided policies in both the surplus and the deficit countries. Forcing only the deficit countries to adjust, he pointed out, is bad for global growth and terrible for the deficit countries. It is also a recipe, he warned, for political instability and extremism. That is not a warning that should be dismissed too quickly.

Germany and the other surplus countries must abandon the policies that forced up their savings rates to artificially high levels. Only in this way can Spanish employment rates, and the employment rates of the other European deficit countries, automatically rise without requiring an abandonment of the euro. The surplus countries, in other words, are as responsible for the terrible European policies as are the deficit countries. They should share the burden of adjustment by reforming their own economic distortions. If Germany does not adjust dramatically, Spain will have no choice but to leave the euro and default on its debt.

The only question is when, and however the crisis is resolved, the adjustment will subsequently be very painful for Germany. This is why it makes sense for Germany to take measures that minimize the cost of the overall adjustment, even if this involves, as it will, slower growth and higher debt for Germany in the short term.

It may seem surprising to argue that Germany—that seeming paragon of thrift and hard work—is at least as vulnerable to the European crisis as Spain, but this would not be the first time in history that a country with relatively low debt and a high trade surplus thought itself invulnerable in the early years of a global demand contraction, only to suffer disproportionately in the end. France, in the early 1930s, was itself in just such a position:

French immunity to the world crisis in 1930 led some commentators to indulge in smug self-congratulation that France would escape the depression. Andre Tardieu, writing just before the fall of his government in December 1930, echoed many analysts in commenting,

One of the reasons for which opinion abroad admires the French people is their resistance to the world economic depression. France's harmonious economic structure and the prompt measures taken by the authorities have facilitated this resistance. The natural prudence of the French people, their ability to adapt, their modernity, and their courage, have contributed equally.[6]

Needless to say, as the world continued to struggle and as France dug itself deeper into the distortions surrounding its domestic monetary policy, conditions quickly changed. Within just a few years the French economy was in shambles and the franc, which the country had struggled so hard to stabilize in the 1920s, was once again forced off gold in a chaotic devaluation.

CHAPTER SEVEN

Foreign Capital, Go Home!

Exporting capital means importing demand, and except in a few restricted and very specific cases, importing capital, especially for rich countries, will mean slower growth and rising unemployment. The "currency wars" that have been much in the news recently are simply "wars" in which countries try desperately to export their unwanted savings to each other.

ONE OF THE BIGGEST WORRIES THAT periodically sweep the international markets is the fear that countries like China, which buy huge amounts of U.S. Treasury bonds, will stop buying U.S. government bonds—perhaps as a way of expressing concern over U.S. creditworthiness or displeasure with U.S. foreign and trade policies. If China stops buying U.S. government bonds, so the argument goes, the U.S. government will be unable to finance itself except with much higher interest rates and much slower growth—perhaps even devolving into crisis.

For example in his February 17, 2009, testimony to Congress, Yale professor and former Morgan Stanley banker Stephen Roach said,

If US-China trade is diminished or closed down through forced RMB revaluation, tariffs, or other means, a saving-short US economy will still need to run a large multi-lateral trade deficit. That means it will simply end up shifting the Chinese piece of its external imbalance to another trading partner. To the extent that shift is directed toward a higher-cost producer—most likely the case—the outcome will be the functional equivalent of a tax hike on the already beleaguered American middle class. But it won't stop there. Undoubtedly, Chinese currency managers would retaliate by reducing their purchases of dollar-denominated assets. And that would push the world's two great powers all the closer to the slippery slope of trade protectionism.[1]

I have already explained, in chapter 5, why a renminbi revaluation will do much more than simply shift the U.S. trade deficit from a Chinese surplus to a Mexican surplus, but the more important point here is that the retaliation by Chinese currency managers, whom Roach worries will reduce their purchases of dollar-denominated assets, is not only very unlikely, but if it were possible it would actually be welcomed by the United States (albeit welcomed much less enthusiastically by whichever country was then forced to supply the alternative assets to China).[2]

It turns out that the fear of a foreign, or Chinese, boycott of U.S. government bond purchases, one of the most common nightmare scenarios bruited about the market, is actually a claim without any real basis and makes little sense for two reasons. First, as we explore in chapter 8, purchases by foreign central banks of U.S. Treasury obligations do not lower U.S. interest rates and do not benefit U.S. growth. If anything, they raise U.S. interest rates by forcing the country to choose between higher debt and higher unemployment. In fact, more generally with a few specific exceptions, countries that export capital do not help the deficit countries that import capital—on the contrary, capital exports often have adverse trade and growth impacts on the recipients.

Second, the decision by countries like China to buy U.S. government obligations is not a discretionary decision that can be made or unmade at will. Remember that the People's Bank of China does not purchase huge amounts of U.S. government bonds simply because it has a lot of money lying around and doesn't know what to do with it. Its purchase of U.S. government bonds is mainly and even exclusively a function of its trade policy.

As we showed in chapter 1, a country cannot run a current account surplus unless it is also a net exporter of capital, and because China runs a large current account surplus and the rest of China (i.e., institutions and individuals other than the central bank) is actually a net importer of capital, the People's Bank of China must export huge amounts of capital, equal to the current account surplus plus other net imports of capital, in order to maintain China's trade surplus. To keep the renminbi from appreciating, the People's Bank of China must be willing to purchase as many dollars as the market offers at the price it sets. It pays for those dollars in renminbi.

It is able to do so by borrowing renminbi in the domestic markets, or by forcing banks to put up minimum reserves on deposit. What does the People's Bank of China do with the dollars it purchases? Because it is such a large buyer of dollars, it must put them in a market that is large enough to absorb the money and—and this is the crucial point—whose economy is willing and able to run a large enough corresponding trade deficit. Remember that the recipient country must see an equivalent deterioration in its trade balance.

In practice, only the U.S. fulfills those two requirements. It has very large and extraordinarily flexible financial markets, and it has the ability and willingness (although perhaps the latter is declining) to run large trade deficits. This is the main, and perhaps only, reason why the People's Bank of China owns huge amounts of U.S. government bonds.

If the People's Bank of China decides that it no longer wants to hold U.S. government bonds, it must do something pretty drastic. There are only four possible paths that the People's Bank of China can follow if it decides to purchase fewer U.S. government bonds.

1.   The People's Bank of China can buy fewer U.S. government bonds and purchase more other U.S. dollar assets

2.   The People's Bank of China can buy fewer U.S. government bonds and purchase more non-U.S. dollar assets, most likely foreign government bonds

3.   The People's Bank of China can buy fewer U.S. government bonds and purchase more hard commodities

4.   The People's Bank of China can buy fewer U.S. government bonds by intervening less in the currency, in which case it does not need to buy anything else

Swapping Assets

We can go through each of these scenarios to see what would happen and what the impact might be on China, the United States, and the world. To make the explanation easier, let's simply assume that the People's Bank of China sells $100 of U.S. government bonds.

The People's Bank of China can sell $100 of U.S. government bonds and purchase $100 of other U.S. dollar assets. In this case basically nothing would happen to the U.S. Treasury bond market. The pool of U.S. dollar savings available to buy U.S. government bonds would remain unchanged (sellers of U.S. dollar assets to China would now have $100, which they would have to invest, directly or indirectly, in U.S. government bonds), China's trade surplus would remain unchanged, and the U.S. trade deficit would remain unchanged.

The only difference might be that the yields on U.S. government bonds will be higher by a tiny amount while credit spreads on risky assets would be lower by the same amount. This will be because there is an increase in the willingness of the market to hold risk assets relative to riskless assets, and the corresponding price of both types of assets will adjust.

The People's Bank of China can sell $100 of U.S. government bonds and purchase $100 of non–U.S. dollar assets, most likely foreign government bonds. Because in principle the only market big enough is Europe, let's just assume that the only alternative is to buy $100 equivalent of euro bonds issued by European governments.

There are two ways the Europeans can respond to the Chinese switch from U.S. government bonds to European bonds. On the one hand they can intermediate Chinese purchases and simply purchase $100 of U.S. dollar assets for themselves. In this case there is no difference to the U.S. government bond market, except that now Europeans instead of Chinese own the bonds. What's more, the U.S. trade deficit will remain unchanged and the Chinese trade surplus also will remain unchanged.

But Europe might be unhappy with this strategy. Because there is no reason for Europeans to buy an additional $100 of U.S. assets simply because China bought euro bonds, the purchase of U.S. dollar assets will probably occur through the European Central Bank, in which case Europe will be forced to accept an unwanted $100 increase in its money supply (the European Central Bank must create euros to buy the dollars).

On the other hand, and for this reason, the Europeans might decide not to purchase $100 of U.S. assets, and this leads to the second way in which Europe can respond. In that case there must be an additional impact. The amount of capital the U.S. imports must decline by $100 and the amount that Europe is importing must rise. Will this reduction in U.S. capital imports make it more difficult to fund the U.S. deficit? No, it will not. On the contrary—it might make it easier, and we will explain why in chapter 8.

But the story doesn't end there. What about Europe? Because China is still exporting $100 by buying European government bonds instead of U.S. government bonds, its trade surplus doesn't change, but of course because the U.S. is importing $100 less, the U.S. trade deficit must decline by that amount. This will impact the European trade account, and if it is running a surplus the European trade surplus must decline by $100. If it is running a trade deficit the deficit must increase by $100.

There are many ways this can happen, but the most likely is that by selling dollars and buying euros, China forces the euro to appreciate against the dollar. As we showed in chapter 2, a stronger euro and a weaker dollar will shift the investment and savings balance in both countries so that a portion of the U.S. trade deficit—$100—must migrate to Europe.

Because demand is already weak in Europe and unemployment high, the deterioration in the European trade account will force Europeans into either raising their fiscal deficits or letting domestic unemployment rise further. Under these conditions it is hard to imagine Europe would tolerate much Chinese purchase of European assets without responding eventually with threats of trade protection. In fact we have already seen countries like Japan and Korea complain loudly when large foreign central banks shift out of dollars and into their currencies, and the European response is likely to be no different.

The People's Bank of China can sell $100 of U.S. government bonds and purchase $100 of hard commodities. This is no different than the above scenario except that now the exporters of those hard commodities must face the choice Europe faced above. Either they can neutralize the trade impact of Chinese purchases by buying U.S. assets or they have to absorb the employment impact of deterioration in their trade account.

This, by the way, is a bad strategy for China but one that it seems nonetheless to be following. Commodity prices are very volatile, and unfortunately this volatility is unstably correlated with Chinese needs. Because China is the largest or second largest purchaser of most commodities, and so has a disproportionate impact on commodity pricing globally, stockpiling commodities is a "profitable" investment only if China continues growing rapidly and pushing commodity prices up further. It is an unprofitable investment if China's growth slows and as a result commodity prices decline.

This is the wrong kind of balance sheet position any county, especially a very poor country like China, should engineer.[3] It simply exacerbates underlying conditions and increases economic volatility—never a good thing—by doubling down on China's underlying position. When it wins, it wins twice, and when it loses it loses twice.

The People's Bank of China can sell $100 of U.S. government bonds by intervening less in the currency, in which case it does not need to buy anything else. In this case, which is the simplest of all to explain, the central bank simply reduces its purchase of dollars, which implies that it allows the renminbi to rise by some amount. Of course as a consequence of the rise in the renminbi China's trade surplus declines by $100 and the U.S. trade deficit declines by $100. The net impact on U.S.

financing costs is unchanged for the reasons to be discussed in chapter 8. Chinese unemployment will rise because of the reduction in its trade surplus unless it increases the fiscal deficit.

It's about Trade, Not Capital

This may sound counterintuitive, but countries that export capital are not doing anyone favors unless incomes in the recipient country are so low or desired investment so high that it is impossible for them to generate sufficient savings to meet their investment needs (like the United States in the nineteenth century) or unless the capital export comes with much-needed technology (like China currently). Countries that import capital under other conditions might be doing so mainly at the expense of domestic jobs or rising debt. For this reason it is unnecessary to worry that China and other foreign countries might stop buying U.S. government bonds.

On the contrary, and we will discuss this further in the next chapter, the whole U.S.-China trade dispute is indirectly about China's insistence on purchasing U.S. government bonds and the U.S. insistence that they stop. How so? Because if the Chinese trade surplus declines, and the U.S. trade deficit declines too, something the United States says it wants, by definition China is directly or indirectly buying fewer U.S. government bonds. This reduction in bond purchases will not cause U.S. interest rates to rise at all. If it were to, it would be like saying that the higher a country's trade deficit, the lower its domestic interest rates. This statement is patently untrue as we will see in the next chapter.

What is ironic is that over the past two years we have become pretty used to the spectacle of Chinese government officials warning the United States about its responsibility to maintain the value of the huge amount of U.S. Treasury bonds the People's Bank of China has accumulated. More recently we have been hearing complaints in Germany about the possibility that defaults in peripheral Europe will lead to losses among the many German banks that hold Greek, Portuguese, Spanish and other European government obligations. In both cases (and many others) there seems to be an aggrieved sense on the part of creditors that after providing so much helpful funding to undisciplined debtors, the creditors are going to be left with losses. There is, they claim, something terribly unfair about the whole thing.

But this argument is a little surreal. Governments do not force their banks or central bank to export capital as a favor to the recipients. They export capital as a way of importing demand and reducing unemployment, usually at the expense of their trade partners. Not only have the creditors totally mixed up the causality of the process, and confused discretionary foreign lending with domestic employment policies, but an erosion in the value of the liabilities owed to them is an almost certain consequence of their own continuing domestic policies, and this is especially likely to be the case for Germany, since the countries to which it has lent money are in such dire straits. It is largely policies in the creditor countries, in other words, that will determine whether or not the value of those obligations must erode in real terms.

Before explaining the second point, let me address the first point. The accumulation of U.S. government bonds by the People's Bank of China and the surging Greek, Portuguese, and Spanish loan portfolios among German banks were not the kindly acts of disinterested lenders. They were simply the automatic consequence of policies in the surplus countries that may very well have been opposed to the best interests of the deficit countries.

This is especially obvious in the case of Germany. As we saw in chapter 6, the strength of the German economy in recent years has largely had to do with its export success, since productivity growth has been negligible. But for Germany to run a large current account surplus—the consequence of domestic policies aimed at suppressing consumption and subsidizing production—the peripheral countries of Europe had to run large current account deficits. If they didn't, the euro would have undoubtedly surged, and with it Germany's export performance would have collapsed. Very low interest rates in the euro area (set largely by Germany) ensured that the peripheral countries would, indeed, run large trade deficits.

The funding by German banks of peripheral European borrowing, in other words, was a necessary part of deal, arrived at willingly or unwillingly, leading both to Germany's export success and to the debt problems of the deficit countries. If the latter behaved foolishly, they could not have done so without equally foolish behavior by Germany, and now both sets of countries—surplus countries and deficit countries—will have to deal jointly with the debt problem.

This makes it illogical for Germans to insist that the peripheral countries have any kind of moral obligation to prevent erosion in the value of the German banks' loan portfolios. It is like saying that they have a moral obligation to accept higher unemployment in order that Germany can reduce its own unemployment. Whether or not these countries default or devalue should be wholly a function of their national interest, and not a function of external obligation, just as German lending was a function of policies aimed at domestic job creation and not acts of European brotherly love.

Trade Imbalances Lead to Debt Imbalances

But aside from whether or not there is a moral obligation for debtor countries to protect the value of portfolios whose accumulation was the consequence of policies that those countries opposed, there is a more concrete reason why it does not make sense to demand that deficit countries act to protect the value of the portfolios accumulated by surplus countries. This has to do with the sustainability of policies aimed at generating trade surpluses. It turns out that the maintenance of the value of those obligations is largely the consequence of trade policies in the surplus countries.

To explain why this is the case, let me simplify matters again, as I did in chapter 6, by calling all surplus countries "Germany" and all deficit countries "Spain." Germany and Spain jointly have put into place policies that ensure that Germany runs a large current account surplus and Spain a large current account deficit for many years.

As demonstrated in chapter 6, as long as Germany runs current account surpluses for many years and Spain the corresponding deficits, it is by definition true there must have been net capital flows from Germany to Spain as German individuals and institutions bought Spanish assets or lent them money to balance the current account imbalances. The capital and current accounts for any country, and for the world as a whole, must balance to zero.

In the old days of specie currency—gold and silver—this meant that specie would have flowed from Spain to Germany as the counterbalancing entry, and of course this flow created its own resolution. Less gold and silver in Spain relative to the size of its economy was deflationary in Spain and more gold and silver in Germany was inflationary there. Spanish prices would have declined and German prices risen to the point where the real exchange rate between the two countries would have adjusted sufficiently to reverse the trade imbalances.

> Early classical thinking was based on the price-specie flow mechanism outlined by David Humes (1752). Gold movements were the instruments by which payments balance was supposed to be achieved. Countries with payments deficit would lose gold, causing an internal price deflation, which would induce a rise in exports and a fall in imports, and the opposite for surplus countries.[4]

Large current account surpluses and deficits, in other words, could not persist because they were limited by the gold and silver holdings of the deficit countries. This was pretty much an automatic limit—although in later centuries it could be extended by central bank loans of specie—and the limit was pretty firm. In the days of Hapsburg Spain, seemingly infinite discoveries of silver in Eastern Europe and the Americas allowed Spain to act as if it had infinite capacity to run deficits, but of course the never-ending religious and dynastic wars that seemed so much to delight the early Hapsburg mentality ensured that silver outflows were high enough to drain even the silver discoveries fairly quickly (in fact new silver discoveries were almost always spent before they were actually delivered).

During the period of imperialism in the late nineteenth century this adjustment mechanism was subverted by a process described most famously by British economist John Hobson in his theory of underconsumption. Hobson argued that the imperial centers systematically underconsumed largely because as wealth was increasingly concentrated among the rich, total consumption was repressed relative to total production.

According to Hobson, as the corresponding rise in domestic savings exceeded domestic investment needs (if domestic consumption is not rising quickly enough, there is little reason to expand domestic manufacturing capacity), the excess savings either would turn to domestic speculation or would flow abroad—generally to real or virtual colonies. As the imperialist centers exported huge amounts of their savings to the colonial periphery, this of course ensured that they would run large and profitable trade surpluses against the periphery.[5]

This export of money from the center to the periphery was seen as the primary mechanism of colonial exploitation. Even Lenin thought so, and wrote about it most famously in *Imperialism, the Highest Stage of Capitalism.*

> Typical of the old capitalism, when free competition held undivided sway was the export of goods. Typical of the latest stage of capitalism, when monopolies rule, is the export of capital.[6]

Exporting capital is of course the same as exporting goods, but the causes are different. Because they controlled the periphery, and because obligations were denominated in gold or silver, the imperial centers exporting capital generally did not have to worry as much about today's worry—the refusal or inability of the periphery to repay the capital imports. They "managed" the colonial economies and their tax systems, and so they could ensure that all debts were repaid. In that case large current account imbalances could persist for as long as the colony had assets to trade.

The Current Account Dilemma

In today's world things are different. There is no adjustment mechanism—specie flow or imperialism—that permits or prevents persistent current account imbalances. This means that if Germany runs persistent trade surpluses with Spain, there are only three possible outcomes.

First, Spain can borrow forever to finance the deficit (of which the ability to sell off national assets is a subset). This may seem like an absurd claim—no country has an unlimited borrowing capacity—but it is not quite absurd. If Germany is very small—say the size of Sri Lanka—or if Germany runs a very small trade surplus, for all practical purposes we can treat the borrowing capacity of Spain as unlimited as long as the growth in debt is more or less in line with Spain's GDP growth. However, if Germany is a large country or runs large surpluses, this clearly is not a possible outcome.

This leaves the other two possible outcomes. First, once Spanish debt levels become worryingly large, Germany and Spain can reverse the policies that led to the large trade imbalances, in which case Germany will begin to run a current account deficit and Spain a current account surplus. In this way German capital flows to Spain can be reversed as Spain pays down those claims with its own current account surplus. Neither side loses.

Second, Spain can take steps to erode the value of those claims in real terms. It can do this by devaluing its currency, by inflating away the value of its external debt, by defaulting on its debt and repaying only a fraction of its original value, by expropriating German assets, or by a combination of these steps.

Why must those claims be eroded? Because if Spain does not have unlimited borrowing capacity (and presumably does not want to give away an unlimited amount of domestic assets), it must settle the debts. If Spain's current account deficit is large enough, in other words, its debt must grow at an unsustainable pace and so it must eventually default. The only way to avoid default is to erode the real value of the debt, and ultimately these are variations on the same thing—Germany will get back in real terms less than it gave.

Without unlimited borrowing capacity these are the only two options, and once the market decides debt levels are too high, a decision must be made. Either Germany must accept a reversal of the current account imbalances or it must accept erosion in the value of the Spanish assets it owns as a consequence of the current account imbalances. This is the important point. Once you have excluded infinite borrowing capacity, there are arithmetically only two other options.

It is pretty clear that the countries of the world represented in my example by Germany (Germany, China, Japan, etc.) are doing everything possible to resist the first option. They are not taking the necessary steps to reverse their anticonsumptionist policies and plan to continue running current account surpluses for many more years. Even Japan, for example, a country that has abandoned its old growth model and has finally been adjusting domestically for nearly two decades, has been unable, or has refused, to take the necessary steps to reverse its current account surplus, and may actually try to increase it in the next few years as it raises consumption taxes to pay down its massive debt.

This means that some mechanism or the other must erode the value of the Spanish assets the German banks have accumulated. Either Spain must devalue, or it must inflate away the real value of the debt, or it must default, or it must appropriate German assets—perhaps in the form of a large German gift to Spain (something akin to, perhaps, the U.S. Marshall Plan).

Given the limits, especially debt limits, it is irrational for anyone to expect that Germany can continue to run large current account surpluses while Spain does nothing to erode the value of Spanish assets held by Germans. This is an impossible combination. We must have either one or the other. Germany is probably hoping and arguing that Spain can somehow reverse its current account deficit without the need for Germany to undermine its current account surplus, but this cannot work except with a much weaker euro, which effectively pushes the problem onto some other country, and it is hard to imagine which other country would not object.

China, by the way, implicitly makes the same argument when it demands that the United States raise its savings rate while China avoids making the necessary domestic adjustments, including to the currency. But of course this means nothing more than that some other country must replace the United States as the current account deficit country of last resort. This obviously cannot solve the underlying problem. It simply pushes off the imbalance onto another country, and ultimately with the same dire consequences.

This is why the moaning and gnashing of teeth over the possible erosion of the value of claims accumulated by surplus countries is fairly surreal. There is only one possible way to avoid that erosion of value, and that requires that the surplus countries work with the deficit countries to reverse the trade imbalances. If the surplus countries refuse to take the necessary steps, erosion in the value of those claims is the automatic and necessary consequence. In practice that means that either the claims must be devalued or they will lead to default.

CHAPTER EIGHT

The Exorbitant Burden

Why do so many countries allow the United States to maintain the exorbitant privilege associated with the world's use of the U.S. dollar as the dominant reserve currency? Because the privilege is minimal and the cost is exorbitant, and the rest of the world needs to acquire dollars in order to acquire a larger share of global demand.

IN THE CLASSIC MARXIST VIEW, CRISES, according to David Harvey, "are, in effect, not only inevitable but also necessary, since this is the only way in which balance can be restored and the international contradictions of capitalist accumulation be at least temporarily resolved." He continued,

> Crises are, as it were, the irrational rationalisers of an always unstable capitalism. During a crisis, such as the one we are now in, it is always important to keep this fact in mind. We have to ask: what is it that is being rationalized here and what directions are the rationalisations taking, since these are what will define not only the manner of exit from the crisis but the future character of capitalism? At times of crisis there are always options.[1]

Over the next few years policymakers and businesses around the world will choose from within the constraints imposed by the global crisis the policies that, as Harvey suggested, will determine the next several decades of economic growth. One of these choices must be about the role of the dollar in international trade and reserve policy.

I claimed in chapter 7 that there were two reasons why the nightmare scenario of a foreign boycott of U.S. government bonds was as lacking in substance as dreams usually are. First, as I explained in chapter 7, the decision by countries like China to buy U.S. government obligations is not discretionary, it cannot be made or unmade at will. A dramatic, and welcome, change in their growth models would be required before they could stop buying U.S. government bonds.

Second, contrary to the widely held assumption, as I argue in the rest of this chapter, purchases by foreign central banks of U.S. Treasury obligations do not lower U.S. interest rates and do not benefit U.S. investment or growth. Consequently, a sharp reduction in foreign purchases of U.S. government bonds would not have the opposite adverse consequences for the economy. The United States, it turns out, not only does not need foreign help in financing its fiscal deficit, but in fact foreign help actually makes the fiscal deficit worse.

Few people seem to understand why this seemingly counterintuitive claim is necessarily true once we consider the workings of the balance of payments. The misunderstanding has even led to some fairly surprising and confused statements by U.S. government officials. In February 2009, for example, newspapers around the world wrote excitedly about how, in the words of one British newspaper, "US Secretary of State Hillary Clinton has pleaded with China to continue buying US Treasury bonds amid mounting fears that Washington may struggle to finance bank bail-outs and ballooning deficits over the next two years."[2]

Secretary Clinton's pleading for loans was unnecessary. However much the United States may struggle over "bank bail-outs and ballooning deficits," Chinese financing help is irrelevant to the process. Before I explain why, it will help if we first take a quick but relevant look at a widely discussed proposal to replace the dollar as the global reserve currency.

For many years countries like France, Germany, Iran, China, Russia, and others have actively promoted the replacement of the U.S. dollar as the dominant reserve currency with an artificial currency or accounting unit issued by the International Monetary Fund. This unit, which consists essentially of a basket of currencies, is known as special drawing rights (SDR).

The debate over the replacement of the dollar by the SDR is often positioned as a struggle between those who want to curtail U.S. economic and political dominance by calling for the replacement of the dollar versus those who support continued U.S. domination of the global economy. As is often the case when seemingly counterintuitive aspects of the global balance of payments come into play, each side seems to have its arguments backward.

First of all, how will the SDR replace the dollar? SDRs are a type of transnational currency whose accounting value is defined in terms of other major currencies. Wikipedia defines it like this:

> Special drawing rights (SDRs) are supplementary foreign exchange reserve assets defined and maintained by the International Monetary Fund (IMF). Not a currency, SDRs instead represent a claim to currency held by IMF member countries for which they may be exchanged.
>
> As they can only be exchanged for euros, Japanese yen, pounds sterling, or U.S. dollars, SDRs may actually represent a potential claim on IMF member countries' non-gold foreign exchange reserve assets, which are usually held in those currencies. While they may appear to have a far more important part to play, or, perhaps, an important future role, being the unit of account for the IMF has long been the main function of the SDR

I argue in this chapter that the SDR, or some reasonably equivalent, should indeed replace the dollar as the dominant reserve currency. This will be an important step toward eliminating the tremendous global trade and capital imbalances that have characterized the world for much of the past one hundred years. The world, however, will not willingly give up the dollar, and so this replacement will not happen until the United States forces the issue—which it seems unwilling to do, perhaps for fear that it would signal a relative decline in the power of the U.S. economy.

But signaling aside, the United States should, in fact, support doing away with the dollar's preeminent role. For all the excited talk of politicians, journalists, and generals, a world without the dollar would mean faster growth and less debt for the United States, although at the expense of slower growth for parts of the rest of the world, especially for Asia. It would not mean that the U.S. government would be unable to fund its deficit. On the contrary, the U.S. fiscal deficit would be smaller and, if anything, easier to fund.

To explain why, it is worth making a quick digression. A French economist once told me that too often, especially in France, when policymakers think they are talking about economics they are actually talking about politics. A case in point, perhaps, is the claim first made in 1965 by Valéry Giscard d'Estaing, when he was France's minister of finance and economic affairs, that the dollar's dominance as the global reserve currency gave the United States an "exorbitant privilege."[3]

Giscard probably thought he was discussing economic privilege, but while during the Cold War there may well have been political advantages to the United States to the use of the dollar as the dominant reserve currency—by generating rapid growth and closer ties with American allies—economically it brought few benefits to the United States. If anything, it forced upon the United States a cost that was small and relatively easy to manage in the 1950s and 1960s, but, with the rapid growth of the rest of the world and the pursuit of export-driven growth in large developing economies, and especially once the dollar was unpegged to gold after the breakdown of the Bretton Woods Agreement, the cost soon became exorbitant.

According to most political commentators, there are two main privileges accruing to the United States as a function of the dollar's reserve status. First, it allows the United States to consume and borrow well beyond its means, as foreigners acquire U.S. dollars in exchange for goods. Second, because foreign governments must buy U.S. government bonds to hold as reserves, this additional source of demand for Treasury bonds lowers U.S. interest rates.[4]

Why Buy Dollars?

Both claims are muddled and even actually wrong. Take the first. It may be correct to say that the role of the dollar as the dominant international reserve currency *allows* Americans to consume beyond their means, but it is just as correct, and probably more so, to say that foreign accumulations of dollars *force* Americans to consume beyond their means.

Can foreign governments really do this? It is easy to dismiss the argument with a snappish "No one puts a gun to the American consumer's head and forces him to consume!" This is, indeed, the standard rejoinder to claims that U.S. overconsumption is at least partly caused by policies abroad, for example in this 2009 op-ed piece:

> It takes two to tango. No one put a gun to the American consumer's head and forced him to buy a new flat-screen TV or to do so by taking out more debt. (Nor are the Chinese somehow morally superior to us; one reason why they save so much more than Americans is that, with no social safety net to speak of, they have to.)[5]

But aside from misunderstanding why the Chinese savings rate is so high (and in fact confusing household savings with national savings), this rejoinder only indicates how confused many people, even economists, are about balance of payments mechanisms and constraints. The external account is not simply a residual of domestic activity, even for a large economy like that of the United States. As I have argued in earlier chapters in this book, it is determined partly by domestic policies and conditions, but also by foreign policies and conditions, which in the latter case directly affects the relationship between domestic American consumption and savings.

How so? When foreign central banks that intervene in their currency are net buyers of dollars—or otherwise repress their domestic financial systems in the ways we discussed in chapters 3 and 4—they automatically increase their savings rate by forcing down household consumption. As their savings rise, the excess must be exported, often in the form of central bank purchases of U.S. government bonds.

By doing so the central banks export those savings onto their trading partners. If there is no change in the total amount of global investment, and because savings must always equal investment, by exporting their savings to the rest of the world, the savings rate of the rest of the world, that is, their trading partners, must decline, whether or not they like it. The only way their trading partners can prevent this is by themselves intervening in trade by directly or indirectly manipulating the relationship between domestic savings and investment—effectively retaliating in the form of a currency war.

This may seem counterintuitive, and it has certainly been hard for many economists to understand, but as we discussed in chapter 5, it is an arithmetical necessity. If a county increases its savings relative to its investment, it must export those savings to the rest of the world. Unless the rest of the world intervenes in trade to prevent the rise in their capital imports, the rest of the world must adjust, and the only two ways it can adjust is by increasing investment or by reducing savings.

This is why when commentators insist that only an internally generated increase in the U.S. savings rate can reduce the trade deficit (and thus it is useless to look abroad for solutions), it is because they do not understand the global balance of payments mechanism. American savings—like those of any open economy—must automatically respond to changes in the global balance of savings and investment.

As counterintuitive as it may seem for such a large economy to be affected by activity abroad, the American response automatically follows from the way the global balance of payments works. To put it in different terms, if foreign central banks intervene in the foreign exchange value of their currencies and, as part of the process, accumulate U.S. dollars, they push down the value of their currency against the dollar and will run current-account surpluses exactly equal to their net purchases of U.S. dollars (or other foreign currency). Purchasing excess amounts of dollars is a policy, in other words, aimed at generating trade surpluses and higher domestic employment.

The reverse is true as well: because its trade partners are accumulating dollars, the United States must run the corresponding current-account deficit, which means that total demand must exceed total production. In this case, it is a tautology that Americans are consuming beyond their means. And it is also a tautology that the rest of the world is underconsuming. One cannot happen without the other, and in principle the causality can run in either or both directions.

Is it possible to discover the direction in which causality was most likely to have run in the past decade? If the imbalance had been initiated by an endogenous consumption binge in the United States, with American investments chasing insufficient and declining domestic savings, we would have expected that rising interest rates in the United States would have been required to pull in savings from abroad to be financed. If the imbalance had been caused by excess savings abroad, which were forcibly exported into the United States in order to divert American demand abroad, we would have expected U.S. interest rates to stay constant or even decline.[6]

Of course too many other factors affect interest rates in the United States for the argument above to be conclusive. In a period however also characterized by tax cuts, foolishly conceived and ruinously expansive military adventures, and rising fiscal deficits, the fact that U.S. interest rates remained broadly stable and even declined during this period of explosive growth in the current account deficit makes it hard to believe that capital inflows were driven wholly or even primarily by endogenous demand and insufficient domestic savings.

It is far more likely that at least part of the reason for the rise in American consumer debt and the decline in American savings was the automatic rebalancing of excess foreign savings. Thanks to the exorbitant privilege, in other words, foreign accumulation of U.S. dollar reserves was counterbalanced partly by an increase in U.S. investment (unfortunately much of which fueling what turned out to be a historically unprecedented real estate bubble) and partly by a reduction in U.S. savings. There are only two ways U.S. savings can decline. One way is to increase U.S. unemployment (as the American tradable goods sector is forced into contraction), and the other way is to increase American debt, which in this case occurred in the form of an increase in consumer debt.

But being forced to choose between unemployment and debt is not a privilege. The sequence of how this happens is quite straightforward. When foreigners actively buy dollar assets, they force down the value of their currency against the dollar, in which case U.S. consumers are subsidized and U.S. manufacturers are penalized by the resulting overvaluation of the dollar. They must reduce production and fire American workers because the expansion of the foreign tradable goods sector relative to foreign demand is necessarily matched with a contraction in the U.S. tradable goods sector relative to domestic demand.

It Is Better to Give Than to Receive

As the American tradable sector contracts, manufacturers must fire workers, and as U.S. unemployment rises, the American savings rate will drop (workers' income will drop faster than their consumption). The only way to prevent unemployment from rising, it turns out, is for the United States to increase domestic demand and expand employment in the nontradable sector by running up public or private debt.

Either the U.S. government must increase its fiscal deficit, in other words, or the Federal Reserve Bank must allow and even encourage private American households and corporations to borrow and spend. With American demand flowing abroad, unfortunately, there was little incentive for American businesses to borrow and expand production domestically, so the only alternative was a rise in domestic consumption fueled, in this case, with surging consumer debt.

There is no way around this fairly mechanical process. If an increase in foreign savings over foreign investment is passed on to the United States by foreign accumulation of dollar assets, unless there is a sharp increase in domestic investment, U.S. savings must decline. And they must decline either by a rise in unemployment or by a rise in consumption. Nothing else is possible.

So where is the privilege in all this? Ask any economist to describe the greatest weaknesses in the U.S. economy and almost certainly the short list will include the gaping trade deficit, low savings level, and high levels of private and public debt. But it is foreign accumulation of U.S. dollar assets that, at best, permits these three conditions (which, by the way, really are manifestations of the same condition) and, at worst, exacerbates and even forces them.

Oddly enough, it seems the whole world realizes this state of play—except perhaps the United States. In late 2011, for example, certain Latin American and Asian central banks began diversifying out of the U.S. dollar, replacing the dollars with purchases of Japanese government bonds. But did Japan think itself lucky to share in the exorbitant privilege that had until then been all but monopolized by the United States? Foreign purchases of bonds, after all, would force up the yen, force down the Japanese trade surplus, and allow Japanese consumption to rise relative to production so that they too could consume beyond their means and use foreign savings to fund their own fiscal debt—which far exceeds that of the United States.

But no, the Japanese authorities failed to see this as a good thing. Whenever foreign purchases of Japanese bonds accelerated, the Bank of Japan intervened heavily, buying U.S. dollar assets as a way of pushing down the value of the yen—effectively converting foreign purchases of yen into foreign purchases of dollars, with the Bank of Japan acting as an intermediary. In February 2012, to take one example, after another period of buying pressure on the yen, in part because of foreign central bank purchases and in part because of generalized risk aversion, the *Financial Times* described the Japanese official reaction:

> Japan has vowed to make unilateral moves to weaken the yen if necessary, in an unusually bold statement of intent. Jun Azumi, finance minister, said on Friday he would "make appropriate decisions at appropriate times on my own," a stance that risks friction with the US, Japan's second-biggest trading partner.
>
> In December the US Treasury Department criticised Japan for its two solo currency interventions in August and October, when it sold yen at times of relatively low market volatility. Mr. Azumi also revealed details of Tokyo's most recent intervention, in a rare example of a senior finance official speaking openly about currency operations by the government and the Bank of Japan.
>
> Mr. Azumi said he had ordered an intervention when the US dollar fell to Y75.63 on October 31, and retreated when the dollar rebounded

to Y78.20. He noted that the currency had remained between Y77 and Y78 until the end of the year. Failing to intervene, he said, could have "caused a critical condition for the Japanese economy."[7]

Or consider this even more revealing story that came out the same time in the *Wall Street Journal*:

How do you get to Tokyo from Beijing? The answer for China's foreign-exchange managers might be: "through London." Data released by Japan's Ministry of Finance on Wednesday shows China reducing its holdings of Japanese debt to the tune of $45 billion in 2011. That makes little sense. China's foreign-exchange reserves grew by some $330 billion last year. Assuming even 3% is allocated to Japan, China's purchases would be at least $10 billion. Given the travails of Europe, China's desire to diversify away from U.S. Treasurys, and the appeal of a rising yen, a higher number seems plausible.

The pattern of China's purchase of U.S. government debt provides a clue to what is going on. The State Administration of Foreign Exchange continues to add to its stock of U.S. Treasurys. But the purchases are often channeled through brokers in London, which means the true extent of China's buying doesn't show up in the U.S. government's regular monthly data. Something similar might be going on with Japan. Like the U.S., the Japanese Ministry of Finance records purchases according to where they are made, not who is making them. Like the data from the U.S., the Japanese numbers show an unaccountably high level of purchases from the U.K.—some $880 billion in 2011. It is impossible to say with certainty, but it is likely that China is behind some of that.

In 2010, Japan's Minister of Finance expressed displeasure at the idea that China could be ramping up its purchase of Tokyo's bonds—fearing the impact it would have on the yen. If China is channeling purchases through London, it might have found a way to benefit from yen appreciation, and diversify its reserves, without risking a spat with its neighbor.[8]

If China is buying Japanese government bonds, according to the author of the article (and indeed to many bond traders), it is doing so secretly in order not to anger Japan. But by acknowledging the adverse impact of foreign purchases of yen, Tokyo seems to have made an enormous about-face. In the 1980s, Japanese policies—including what many in the United States and Europe believed was a sharply undervalued yen buttressed by massive purchases of U.S government bonds—corresponded with enormous trade surpluses for Japan, along with the corresponding current account deficits for the United States.

At the time Japanese policymakers (and many American and European economists, too) insisted—like Beijing policymakers today in the Chinese context (and again like many American and European economists)—that Japan's trade surplus was primarily a consequence of the underlying competitiveness of its industry, its cultural propensities toward hard work and thrift, and perhaps most impressively its farsighted economic planning and policymaking.

The currency regime, Tokyo and its allies argued, had at best a small, and largely short-term, impact on the trade imbalances, which were driven, above all, by fundamental differences in economic abilities. "While the US has been busy creating lawyers," Akio Morita, cofounder of Sony, famously explained in his 1986 best-selling autobiography, *Made in Japan*, "we have been busy creating engineers."

Twenty years later Japanese officials seem to have changed their minds about the relevance of the yen's exchange value as well as the exorbitant privileges that accrue to central bank reserve status. The value of the currency, they have decided, does indeed matter to a country's international competitiveness, and when the People's Bank of China or other foreign central banks and investors acquire enough Japanese government bonds to drive up the yen, the Bank of Japan regularly retaliates or unwinds the purchases by purchasing U.S. government bonds, thus intermediating unwanted foreign capital exports to Japan onto the United States.

Japanese authorities, in other words, consistently refuse to accept any part of the exorbitant privilege that many believe to be one of the great unfair sources of economic power for the United States. And it is not just the Japanese. For all its stated desire to have the renminbi acquire global reserve status, China restricts foreign purchases of government bonds, while more open countries, from South Korea to Brazil, regularly fulminate at and interfere with foreign attempts to acquire domestic bonds for trade purposes. Whenever they are offered a portion of the exorbitant privilege, they insist on handing it back to Americans.

Consuming beyond your means, it seems, is not much of a blessing. And why should it be? Allowing excessive foreign purchases of its bonds requires often that the reserve currency country choose between rising unemployment and rising debt.

Foreigners Fund Current Account Deficits, Not Fiscal Deficits

What about the second of the two benefits of the exorbitant privilege—doesn't the huge amount of foreign purchases of U.S. government bonds at least aid the U.S. government in financing its enormous fiscal deficit, and doesn't it cause interest rates to be lower than they otherwise would have been? After all, any increase in demand for bonds (assuming no change in supply) should cause bond prices to rise and, with it, interest rates to fall.

But of course this claim implicitly assumes that there is no concomitant rise in supply, and here is where the claim falls apart. Remember that foreign purchases of the dollar force up the value of the dollar, and so undermine U.S. manufacturers.

This should cause a rise in unemployment. As we pointed out earlier in this chapter the only way for the United States to attempt to reduce this level of joblessness is to increase its private consumer financing or its public borrowing. It can also increase business borrowing for investment purposes, but this is unlikely to happen when the manufacturing sector is being undermined by a strong dollar.

This is just another way of saying that in order to maintain full employment, the supply of U.S. dollar bonds must rise with the increased foreign demand for U.S. dollar bonds. Purchases by foreigners of U.S. debt, in other words, are matched by additional debt issued by Americans. But, in this case, interest rates will not decline. The domestic supply of bonds rises as fast as foreign demand for bonds.

What if you believe, as most economists do, that trade is a more efficient way to create jobs than government spending or consumer financing? If you're right the amount of additional American debt issued to keep unemployment constant in that case will actually exceed net foreign purchases, in which case increased foreign purchases of U.S. dollar debt may paradoxically cause U.S. interest rates to rise.

How so? Because if a $1 improvement in the trade balance is a more efficient way to increase employment than a $1 increase in the fiscal deficit, then any $1 increase in the U.S. current account deficit will require an increase in the fiscal deficit of more than $1 to keep unemployment stable. Foreigners will lend the United States $1, but American debt will have grown by more than $1.

Foreigners, it must be remembered, do not fund fiscal deficits. They fund current account deficits, and they do so automatically. Under many if not most conditions the impact of a rising current account deficit is lower tax receipts (workers are fired and business profits fall) and higher fiscal expenditures (unemployed workers get compensation, and the government expands fiscally to keep unemployment down). The net result is that foreign purchases of U.S. government bonds increase the supply of U.S. government bonds. Americans do not benefit from foreign largesse.

Confused? There's an easier way of thinking about it. By definition, any increase in net foreign purchases of U.S. dollar assets must be accompanied by an equivalent increase in the U.S. current account deficit. So if foreign central banks increase their currency intervention by buying more U.S. dollars, their current account surplus necessarily rises, along with the U.S. current account deficit. This makes it very easy to determine which government receives the most "help" from foreign investors.

The math is simple. The larger a country's current account deficit as a share of GDP, the more "help" that country's government gets from foreign investors to buy its bonds.[9] Of course the opposite is true too. The larger a country's current account surplus, the more money is taken out of the pool available for buying domestic government bonds.

But if foreign purchases of dollar assets really result in lower U.S. interest rates, then it should hold true for all countries, in which case the higher a country's current account deficit, the lower its interest rate should be. If the United States wanted to increase the amount of U.S. Treasury bonds that foreign central banks purchased by $100 billion, to put it in a different way, all it would need to do is engineer a $100 billion increase in the U.S. current account deficit.

Conversely, if foreign purchases of government bonds lowered a country's interest rate, the higher a country's current account surplus, the higher its interest rates should be. Why? Because of the need for the capital and current accounts to balance: the net amount of foreign purchases of U.S. government bonds and other U.S. dollar assets is exactly equal to the current account deficit. A larger number of net foreign purchases is exactly the same as a wider trade deficit (or, more technically, a wider current account deficit).

Rebalancing the Scales

So do bigger trade deficits really mean lower interest rates for the deficit country, and do bigger trade surpluses mean higher interest rates for the surplus country? Clearly not. The opposite is in fact far more likely to be true. Countries with balanced trade or trade surpluses tend to enjoy lower, not higher, interest rates on average than countries with large current account deficits—and this is probably because countries with very large trade deficits (and lots of foreign buyers of their assets) are handicapped by slower growth and higher debt.

The point here is that unless countries are capital poor, or unless their governments are perceived as being uncreditworthy, their governments are always able fully to finance themselves domestically. Foreign financing must come with a trade or current account deficit, and the foreign funding either goes to fund higher domestic investment or is matched by an increase in local public or private debt.

The United States, it turns out, does not need foreign purchases of government bonds to keep the lights on or to keep interest rates low, any more than it needs a large trade deficit to do either (and of course these two statements mean the same thing). Unless the United States were starved for capital, or starved of the foreign technology that foreign capital might bring, savings and investment would balance just as easily and perhaps even more efficiently without a trade deficit as with one.

Because this point is so counterintuitive for many economists and commentators, and flies in the face of comments repeated thousands of times in the press by seemingly knowledgeable experts, it bears repeating. Rich counties like the United States (and Europe for that matter) do not need foreign help in funding domestic borrowing needs. Net foreign borrowing funds the debt or investment associated with the current account deficit—nothing more.

But what about the countries of peripheral Europe? With European leaders begging the Chinese, Brazilian, and other well-stocked central banks to bail them out, doesn't this prove that rich countries do indeed need help to fund their fiscal deficits?

No, it just proves that they have no credibility. The problem of Spain and the rest of peripheral Europe is not that Europe lacks capital with which to buy their government bonds, but rather that Europeans do not want to lend them money for fear that they will default. If this were merely a problem of lack of capital, it would be easy to resolve to the content of all major parties. China can lend money to Germany and Germany can then lend it to Spain.

Berlin, however, really doesn't need Chinese money to do so. If Germany and Europe's other creditworthy sovereigns simply took the expedient of guaranteeing all Spanish debt, we would quickly see that Spain would have no trouble financing itself with European capital. Europe, it turns out, is capital rich and has more than enough capital domestically. In fact Europe and especially Germany have been net exporters of capital for many years.

So the problem is not lack of capital but rather that Berlin does not want to take on Spanish risk, mainly because it believes that the chances of a Spanish default are too high, and that guaranteeing Spanish obligations would undermine German's own creditworthiness. What Berlin really wants is for someone else to lend to Spain and so take on the risks of a Spanish default. Not surprisingly, the People's Bank of China and other developing-country central banks are not especially eager to comply.

And what would happen if the Europeans anyway did indeed convince the People's Bank of China to lend money to Spain? If Beijing financed these loans by selling the German bonds it owns in its portfolio, there would be no net change in European liquidity, but a significant increase in the riskiness of the assets owned by the People's Bank of China.

But if Beijing financed these new loans to Madrid by selling U.S. dollar bonds, there would certainly be an increase in the total amount of funds available to fund European government debt, but—and here's the rub—there would be an equal or even greater increase in the amount of European debt that needed to be funded. Europe's debt burden would rise as fast as or faster than the additional foreign capital available to fund it.

Why? Because the capital and current account must balance. A net increase in capital flows into Europe must be matched by a reduction in the European current account surplus or an increase in its current account deficit—probably because the Chinese swap of dollar bonds for euro bonds would cause the euro to rise against the dollar, which would slow European exports and increase European imports. The weaker net external demand would cause European growth to slow, European unemployment to rise, and European fiscal deficits to surge by an amount equal to or even greater than the amount of Chinese inflows.

With Chinese funding of European debt, Europe, ironically, would find itself enjoying part of the supposed benefits of exorbitant privilege. It would discover however that while more foreign funding sounds like a good thing, it is the same as larger current account deficits, which most certainly are not a good thing for countries struggling with low demand, weak growth, and rising unemployment.

When Are Net Capital Inflows a Good Thing?

The discussion about foreign financing of peripheral Europe leads to an interesting question. If it is true, as we have argued, that net flows of capital from one country to another in most cases force the recipient to choose between higher debt and higher unemployment, there should nonetheless be cases in which net inflows are good. If so, under what conditions do net capital inflows improve long-term growth prospects, and under what conditions do they undermine growth or raise debt?

It turns out that there are for the most part three conditions under which net foreign capital inflows improve long-term growth prospects for the recipient country:

1. When a country has high levels of potentially productive investment but domestic savings are insufficient to satisfy domestic demand, the country benefits from importing foreign capital to fund those productive investments. As long as the total economic return on these investments, including all externalities, exceeds the cost of the foreign borrowing, or is funded by foreign equity investment, foreign capital inflows are wealth creating for the recipient.

    On of the classic examples is the United States for much of the nineteenth century. During that period, as the American economy and domestic consumer markets expanded dramatically, total American savings were insufficient to fund the wide range of profitable investment opportunities.

    Part of the reason for insufficient savings may have been the combination of native optimism and good long-term growth, which together kept consumption rates higher than they might otherwise have been, but a more important reason may have been the immaturity and riskiness of the American monetary and financial system. Americans were distrustful of banks, and with good reason, because they often engaged in speculative behavior and in many cases defaulted on their deposit obligations, so when Americans did save they often did so by investing in land or hoarding specie.

Whatever the reason, for long periods of time there was an insufficiently large capital base to satisfy the tremendous investment opportunities in the country, and the United States had to turn to foreign funding, especially British and Dutch funding, to satisfy investment. Of course with net capital inflows to fund domestic investment, the United States ran current account deficits for much of this period, but the wealth generated by foreign-funded investment was more than enough to repay the foreign debt and equity obligations. In that case foreign capital inflows were positive both for the world and for the United States. Without it European savers would have earned a lower return on their savings, European manufacturers would have had fewer clients, and American wealth would have grown more slowly.

2. When major borrowers, including the government, face severe short-term liquidity constraints and domestic capital is, for whatever reason, unwilling or unable to fund maturing debt, foreign capital inflows can help bridge the gap. In this case foreign investors fulfill the classic role of a central bank, lending to creditworthy borrowers or against acceptable assets in order to prevent a liquidity crisis from forcing the borrower into insolvency.

This is the basic argument as to why Europe should turn to China and other foreign lenders to fund the maturing obligations of governments of countries like Spain. According to this reasoning, Spain does not have a solvency problem, but for reasons that may or may not be rational, European investors are unwilling to lend money to Spain. In that case large loans from foreign central banks, even if they cause a temporary worsening of the current account balance, can prevent an unnecessary bankruptcy, which would certainly be disorderly and would create huge financial distress costs for the economy over the longer term.

3. For countries that lack technology, that have weak business and management institutions, or that suffer from low levels of social capital,

foreign investment can bring with it the technology and management skills that allow the economy to grow faster than its foreign debt and equity obligations.

Aside from under these three obvious conditions, net foreign inflows of capital are unlikely to generate long-term wealth for an economy. On the contrary, if foreign inflows fund consumption or speculative investments, for example in real estate, they can easily be wealth destroying in the aggregate since the increase in real wealth creation in the recipient economy is less than the increase in debt servicing cost.

Notice that these three conditions are generally likely to characterize poor or rapidly growing countries, countries devastated by war or natural disasters, or countries heavily reliant on commodity extraction. Rich, diversified economies with sophisticated financial systems almost never need net foreign funding, and it is certainly hard to make the argument in the case of the United States that the American capital markets are insufficiently sophisticated, capable of taking risk, or knowledgeable to fund the astonishing creativity of U.S. technology. If the United States is a net importer of capital, it is almost certainly likely to result in excess consumption or asset bubbles (and the latter usually feeds the former in the way described in chapters 2 and 3).

Can We Live without the Dollar?

In fact until the final breakdown of the gold standard, and excluding periods in which countries were rebuilding after the devastation of war—for example Germany and Japan in the 1950s, or Belgium in the 1920s—rich manufacturing countries have usually been net exporters of capital, with poor countries or rapidly growing countries usually the net importers, with all the positives identified by classic trade theory and all the negatives identified by John Hobson and Vladimir Lenin (which we discussed in chapter 7). Mature, rich, diversified countries, in other words, have never needed foreign funding.

But when these countries did receive large capital inflows that were not associated with burgeoning productive investment at home—the obvious examples being the United States and peripheral Europe in the past decade—the nearly automatic result was that the recipient country was forced to choose between rising unemployment or an unsustainable increase in debt. Without some automatic adjustment mechanism preventing the strategic accumulation of dollar reserves or local assets by other countries, large imbalances could persist in ways that would have been impossible earlier.

This was a problem for the United Kingdom after the 1914–18 war, when the world seemed to shift from a more or less hard gold standard to a sterling exchange standard, and for the United States after the 1939–45 war, when it shifted to a dollar exchange standard, and especially after the collapse of the Bretton Woods Agreement in 1971. Perhaps the change should not have been a surprise. The breakdown of Bretton Woods eliminated one of the classic adjustment mechanisms—the need to back money creation with gold—that prevented countries from accumulating unlimited amounts of foreign reserves, and it was only afterward that it became possible for countries that normally should have been net capital importers to reverse positions with countries that normally should have been net capital exporters.

This is certainly not to say that we were better off under the gold standard, but it does suggest that some of the automatic adjustment mechanisms under the gold standard were extremely useful and should somehow be replicated. Perhaps the SDR, or some functional equivalent, can do just that by spreading reserve accumulation among a wide group of capital recipients. The world, after all, needs something like the dollar. The fact that the global trading and investing communities have a widely available and very liquid reserve and trade currency is a common good, but like all common goods, it can be exploited or gamed.

When countries use the dollar's reserve status to gain trade advantage by accumulating reserves, the United States suffers economically—without any of the supposed benefit of exorbitant privilege. What's worse, the greater the subsequent trade imbalances, the more fragile the global financial system will be and the likelier a financial collapse. Even the country gaming the system, like Japan in the 1980s, ultimately suffers from the imbalances that were created at least in part by their strategic accumulation of dollar reserves.

If the world is to address these global imbalances, it cannot do so without addressing the part that currency intervention and accumulation play. Some seventy years ago, John Maynard Keynes tried to get the world to understand this when he argued in favor of the creation of Bancor, a supranational currency to be used in international trade as a unit of account within a multilateral barter clearing system. Because of obstinate (and now clearly misguided) American opposition, he failed to win his argument, of course, and we have been living ever since with the consequences.

But perhaps things are improving. On the surface, it looks like the world is starting to understand the reserve currency mess. Still, too much muddled thinking dominates. For example, government officials in many countries talk increasingly about promoting SDRs as an alternative to the dollar, but much of the reasoning behind it is bureaucratic thinking. The world doesn't hold more SDRs, their argument goes, largely because there isn't a better formal mechanism to create more SDRs. Fix the latter and the former will be resolved.

This recent form of the debate was kicked off in March 23, 2009, by Governor Zhou Xiaochuan of the People's Bank of China. In an essay on the reform of the international monetary system published on the central bank's website,[10] and which generated an enormous amount of interest in the months following its publication, Zhou started with,

> The outbreak of the current crisis and its spillover in the world have confronted us with a long-existing but still unanswered question, i.e., what kind of international reserve currency do we need to secure global financial stability and facilitate world economic growth, which was one of the purposes for establishing the IMF? There were various institutional arrangements in an attempt to find a solution, including the Silver Standard, the Gold Standard, the Gold Exchange Standard

and the Bretton Woods system. The above question, however, as the ongoing financial crisis demonstrates, is far from being solved, and has become even more severe due to the inherent weaknesses of the current international monetary system.

Of course he was correct. He then went on to argue that the existing system, dependent as it is on the U.S. dollar and American monetary and credit policies, was inherently instable. The solution?

Though the super-sovereign reserve currency has long since been proposed, yet no substantive progress has been achieved to date. Back in the 1940s, Keynes had already proposed to introduce an international currency unit named "Bancor," based on the value of 30 representative commodities.

Unfortunately, the proposal was not accepted. The collapse of the Bretton Woods system, which was based on the White approach, indicates that the Keynesian approach may have been more farsighted. The IMF also created the SDR in 1969, when the defects of the Bretton Woods system initially emerged, to mitigate the inherent risks sovereign reserve currencies caused. Yet, the role of the SDR has not been put into full play due to limitations on its allocation and the scope of its uses. However, it serves as the light in the tunnel for the reform of the international monetary system.

A super-sovereign reserve currency not only eliminates the inherent risks of credit-based sovereign currency, but also makes it possible to manage global liquidity. A super-sovereign reserve currency managed by a global institution could be used to both create and control the global liquidity. And when a country's currency is no longer used as the yardstick for global trade and as the benchmark for other currencies, the exchange rate policy of the country would be far more effective in adjusting economic imbalances. This will significantly reduce the risks of a future crisis and enhance crisis management capability.

Why Not Use SDRs?

Governor Zhou also seemed to imply that the problems preventing widespread adoption of SDRs were mostly functional. The recommendations in his essay:

> Set up a settlement system between the SDR and other currencies. Therefore, the SDR, which is now only used between governments and international institutions, could become a widely accepted means of payment in international trade and financial transactions.

> Actively promote the use of the SDR in international trade, commodities pricing, investment and corporate book-keeping. This will help enhance the role of the SDR, and will effectively reduce the fluctuation of prices of assets denominated in national currencies and related risks.

> Create financial assets denominated in the SDR to increase its appeal. The introduction of SDR-denominated securities, which is being studied by the IMF, will be a good start.

> Further improve the valuation and allocation of the SDR. The basket of currencies forming the basis for SDR valuation should be expanded to include currencies of all major economies, and the GDP may also be included as a weight. The allocation of the SDR can be shifted from a purely calculation-based system to a system backed by real assets, such as a reserve pool, to further boost market confidence in its value

Many analysts interpreted Zhou's essay as an attack on U.S. dominance of the global monetary system, and suggested that the governor was using the crisis as a way of breaking free from the shackles imposed upon China and the world by U.S. insistence that the world use the dollar. Whatever Zhou's intention, however, this interpretation of his essay reflected a total misunderstanding of the global balance of payments mechanism.

Neither constraints on the availability and functionality of SDRs nor U.S. power explains the dominance of the U.S. dollar as the global currency. Conspiracy theories notwithstanding, these are not the reason why the world's central banks don't hold SDRs. After all, if any large central bank, like that of China, Japan, France, Russia, or Brazil, wanted to buy SDRs, or effectively take on SDR exposure, it would not be hard for it to do so. All a central banker would need to do is check Wikipedia for the formula that sets the currency components of the SDR and then mimic the formula in its own reserve accumulation. The formula is no secret.

But most of the world's largest holders of U.S. dollars as reserves will never do this, and the reason is because of the automatic trade constraints. By buying SDRs, or its currency equivalent, central banks are implicitly spreading their reserve accumulation away from dollars and into those other currencies. In doing so, any country that tries to generate large trade surpluses by accumulating reserves would be forcing the corresponding deficit not just onto the U.S. economy, but also onto those of other countries (according to the currency component in the SDR).

Europe, Japan, and any other country whose currency is accepted into the SDR have made it very clear, however, that they would oppose these kinds of trade practices and would not allow their currencies to rise because of foreign accumulation. A few days after the Zhou essay, I wrote on my blog, *China Financial Markets*,[11]

The number one topic of conversation right now seems to be an essay posted in both English and Chinese on the PBoC's website by PBoC Governor Zhou Xiaochuan. In it Governor Zhou argues that the world needs a new and better reserve currency, one not dominated by a single country, and that it is in the best interest of the world that this reserve currency be created by a body like the IMF.

We have heard these kinds of arguments many times before over the course of the 20th century, and usually in response to a global balance of payments crisis. Is there anything new about this proposal? Some commentators saw this essay as a purely political move. Jamil Anderlini of the *Financial Times*, for example, had this to report:

Analysts said the proposal was an indication of Beijing's fears that actions being taken to save the domestic US economy would have a negative impact on China. "This is a clear sign that China, as the largest holder of US dollar financial assets, is concerned about the potential inflationary risk of the US Federal Reserve printing money," said Qu Hongbin, chief China economist for HSBC.

Although Mr. Zhou did not mention the U.S. dollar, the essay gave a pointed critique of the current dollar-dominated monetary system. Others were more intrigued by the theoretical implications of the essay. A number of people including Columbia University's Joseph Stiglitz, are supportive of the idea, arguing that the status of the U.S. dollar as the world's reserve currency creates unnecessary problems for both the U.S. and the rest of the world.

Most importantly for the U.S. it means that it is very difficult for the Fed to manage domestic monetary policy because the U.S. financial system must accommodate not only conditions in the United States but also distortions introduced by the use of the U.S. dollar as a reserve currency, and these distortions can be massive. The most obvious example is the way over the past decade systematic industrial policies mainly in China and East Asia aimed at running trade surpluses and the accumulation of reserves meant that the U.S. economy and its financial and monetary systems were forced to adjust in ways that created large and serious imbalances, which only now are we resolving.

An American Push Away from Exorbitant Privilege

Without tremendous pressure from the United States to limit the ability of foreign central banks to accumulate dollars, I was very skeptical about the future of the SDR. My post continued,

But although I think the world would be better off if there were an active alternative to the U.S. dollar, I can't help but think all this flurry of talk is a waste of time and driven mainly by political considerations almost wholly divorced from any understanding of exactly what a reserve currency is and how its status is achieved. Every one or two decades there seem to be calls for the replacement of the U.S. dollar with a more international reserve "currency" but they always lead exactly nowhere, and I can't think of any reason why this time will be different. On the contrary, one of my working assumptions is that with the end of the global liquidity cycle the value of liquidity will be higher than ever. New currencies and currency unions (like the euro, by the way) thrive during the liquidity cycle. They almost never survive the end of the cycle.

Perhaps Governor Zhou has much more faith than I do in the role policymakers have in creating reserve status—as if you could check a few boxes, make a political decision, and then simply create a new, widely used reserve currency. But the fact is that excessive reliance on the U.S. dollar was not a policy decision. If the world truly wants a more "balanced" reserve currency system there are, after all, many currencies that could have functioned alongside the U.S. dollar, but investors, central banks, and international traders seem to have had little interest in acquiring a "balanced" portfolio of reserve currencies.

Why? For one thing liquidity is key, and I think not even the euro—and certainly not SDRs or alternatives to the SDR—can ever hope to achieve anything like the level of liquidity implicit in the U.S. dollar market. For another thing, for a currency to achieve reserve status there must be some systematic way of delivering the currency to central banks and other players who want to acquire it, and the U.S. does so by its ability and willingness to run persistent trade deficits and open capital accounts. How will the IMF or whoever controls the SDR create and assign reserves?

Specifically, if the SDR is indeed a true reserve currency, and not simply an accounting entry that allows central banks to pretend that they are not holding dollars but whose value ultimately rests on its convertibility to the U.S. dollar, who will determine the global money supply and how do we prevent this from becoming a horribly politicized process? After all the Fed has an interest in seeing stability in the value and use of the dollar, and so it can be counted on more or less to act in the best interest of the reserve currency, but why should anyone care about the value of the SDR over the long term and, more importantly, how can prudent behavior be enforced?

More worryingly, if Europe has had so much trouble managing monetary policy among a group of neighboring countries with fairly similar social and economic conditions, how do we manage monetary policy on a global scale?

Perhaps the SDR is a covert way of getting back to something resembling the gold standard by creating a fiat currency with very strict rules about its expansion.

If that is the case, the SDR almost certainly won't last long. Since we've gone off the gold standard we have forgotten how brutal and unforgiving gold-standard discipline can be, and I think it was Barry Eichengreen who argued in his magisterial *Golden Fetters* that the gold standard could only work in a society in which workers have little political power, the voting franchise is limited, and the impact of monetary policies on underlying economic conditions was not widely understood.[12]

I went on to argue that the world accumulates dollars rather than SDRs for one very simple reason. Only the U.S. economy and financial system are large enough, open enough, and flexible enough to accommodate large trade deficits. But that badge of honor comes at a real cost to the long-term growth of the domestic U.S. economy and its ability to manage debt levels.

Without a significant reform in the way countries are permitted to hold U.S. dollar assets, there cannot be a meaningful reform of the global economy. If the SDR is truly to replace the dollar as the dominant reserve currency, it will not happen simply because there is a more robust institutional framework around the existence of the SDR. It will happen only because the world, or more likely the United States, creates rules that prevent countries from accumulating U.S. dollars.

Will this happen any time soon? Probably not. Washington is strongly opposed to any reduction in the role of the dollar as the world's reserve currency, even though that would benefit the U.S. economy, and countries like China, Japan, South Korea, Russia, and Brazil will never voluntarily give up the trade advantages of hoarding dollars. But at the very least, economists might want to clear a few things up—perhaps starting by abolishing the phrase "exorbitant privilege."

CHAPTER NINE

When Will the Global Crisis End?

If the great trade and capital imbalances of the previous de-cade caused the global crisis, the crisis cannot be said to have ended until these imbalances are reversed. Although we are seeing some adjustment, in general the global economy has barely adjusted in the aggregate. One of the consequences of this failure to adjust will be worsening trade tensions.

IN THIS BOOK I HAVE TRIED to put together as logically as possible a number of points, often counterintuitive, that follow from the standard balance of payments and macroeconomic accounting identities. Accounting identities are true by definition, of course, and cannot plausibly be disputed, so to the extent these points follow logically, they must be valid. To summarize,

1. A country's savings level is not only or even primarily a function of domestic cultural and personal preferences. Savings rates, especially in countries with abnormally high or low levels of savings, are almost always determined by policies and institutional constraints that affect the relationship between consumption levels and GDP.

2. For relatively open economies, national savings rates are a function not just of domestic policies and institutional constraints but also, and very importantly, of foreign policies and institutional constraints. A low savings rate at home for an open economy is as likely to be caused by conditions that force up consumption at home as by conditions that force up savings abroad. This is less true for closed economies.

3. Policies or conditions that cause household income or household wealth to grow faster than GDP will tend to reduce the savings rate by forcing up consumption relative to GDP. When household income growth is constrained relative to GDP growth, however, the savings rate usually rises.

4. Anything that affects the gap between domestic investment and domestic savings will automatically have a trade impact. It does not matter at all whether the policy is intended to affect trade.

5. Through the trade impact it must also automatically affect in an equal but opposite way the gap between foreign investment and foreign savings.

6. For these reasons, attempts to adjust large savings, consumption, or investment imbalances levels in only one country, without equivalent and opposite adjustments abroad, can force undue stress on the global economy and can lead to very poor outcomes, especially at first for deficit countries but ultimately more so for surplus countries.

7. Exporting capital is the same as importing demand.

8. Large-scale net capital imports can be positive for recipient countries under certain very specific conditions, but otherwise they are usually harmful. Countries receiving growing net capital imports have no choice but to respond to the growing net inflows with higher investment, higher unemployment, or higher consumption (which must occur either as declining savings or as an unsustainable increase in debt). There is no other possibility.

9. For rich, credible countries with diversified economies, foreign capital inflows do not lower government borrowing costs. The U.S. government, in other words, does not benefit from lower interest rates by foreign reserve accumulation, although the nature of the reserve accumulation may affect the shape of the domestic yield curve.

10. Although there are huge advantages to the world having a liquid and easily traded common currency, there are also huge risks if there are no mechanisms in place that prevent reserve accumulation

or other forms of capital exports from becoming excessive, and so destabilizing.

11. The role of the U.S. dollar as the global reserve currency does not create for the United States an exorbitant privilege. It is more likely to suffer from an exorbitant burden

These points have very important policy and economic implications. For one, if it is true that the global crisis is largely a function of the domestic financial distortions and imbalances caused or reinforced by the great global trade and capital imbalances, it would be meaningless to proclaim the end of the crisis until the underlying imbalances have either been worked out or are reduced to sustainable levels. Is this happening?

In 2008 I argued that given the structure and depth of the imbalances and the steps needed for a rebalancing to take place, the crisis would spread from the United States to the rest of the world. I also argued that the United States would probably be the first country to get through the necessary deleveraging process—albeit very painfully—and so the first county to emerge from the crisis.

China, on the other hand, I thought would be the last major economy to emerge from the crisis. It seemed to me that the domestic distortions that were part of the global imbalances were entrenched more deeply within the Chinese growth model, and I worried that China's less robust and flexible political mechanisms—which have been much discussed recently in China in the debate over "vested interests" and after the spectacular fall in early 2012 of Chongqing's former mayor, Bo Xilai—would cause necessary reforms to be postponed.

Transferring the Center of the Crisis

At first the prediction that China would be the last major economy to emerge from the crisis seemed to many analysts, at best, eccentric. The United States was clearly in the throes of a deep recession and rising unemployment, and Europe was struggling with its own debt and currency problems, whereas Beijing responded to the crisis with a massive bank-financed increase in investment of over 30 percent of GDP that allowed China to barge through the global crisis with GDP growth rates of 9 percent and more.

So successful did Chinese anticrisis policies seem that the rest of the world marveled, sometimes in an uncomprehending way, at Beijing's forceful response. The massive investment boom of 2009 and 2010 was hailed as a corrective to the global meltdown, and many commentators even argued that China would remain unscathed by the crisis.

As late as January 2012, for example, a Dutch academic wrote an article in *Foreign Policy* in which she both blamed Beijing as the main culprit behind the global and the European crisis (German behavior was exempted on the erroneous grounds that German foreign loans were qualitatively different from China's accumulation of central bank reserves) and claimed that China would remain unaffected by the resolution of the U.S. and European imbalances. More confusingly, the author predicted that many years of strong growth in China over the rest of the decade would help pull the world out of the crisis:

> Economic growth in the emerging economies will likely go a long way toward buoying the global economy this decade. Apple recently experienced firsthand how ferocious Asian consumers' appetite can be when near riots broke out at its flagship store in Beijing after it postponed the launch of the iPhone 4S due to crowd size.
>
> . . . . As China's economy continues to mature, it may just be the economic engine that the United States and Europe need to dig themselves out from under their mountain of debt.[1]

This argument doesn't make sense for at least two reasons. First, and this is an extraordinarily widespread misunderstanding, for China to be meaningfully an engine for global growth, it is not enough merely to be the highest arithmetical component of global growth. The world needs more demand, and countries with large trade surpluses are net absorbers of global demand, not engines of growth. It is not high Chinese growth rates that will help the world, in other words. It is Chinese rebalancing of the gap between domestic savings and domestic investment that will create growth for the world, with or without high Chinese growth rates. Only when China is importing capital and exporting demand will it be a net contributor to growth abroad.

Second, and more bizarrely, the author asserts a causal link between domestic Chinese distortions and the rest of the world that works powerfully in one direction but seems to disappear in the other direction. If Chinese policy distortions played a role in creating the global imbalances, however—and clearly they have, although not perhaps to the extent that the author suggests—as the rest of the world adjusts it must force an equivalent and opposite adjustment within China itself. As the United States and Europe "dig themselves out from under their mountain of debt," in other words, their deleveraging cannot take place without affecting the gap between Chinese savings and investment.

The global balance of payments, after all, must balance. An increase in savings relative to investment in the rest of the world must either force up Chinese investment or force down Chinese savings. If Beijing is serious about bringing down investment levels over the next few years, as it claims to be, then deleveraging abroad will force China to reduce domestic savings dramatically, something it has been unable to do for many years and in which it can succeed only with great difficulty and serious reform.

One very unwelcome way to lower the Chinese savings rate, of course, is in the form of rising unemployment, but even if China is able to keep unemployment low, deleveraging abroad will force China to grow in a very different way. To claim that China can remain unaffected by the crisis-linked rebalancing of the global imbalances, of which it was a major component, simply does not make sense.

In fact more generally any claim that certain major developing countries, like Brazil, have managed to avoid being derailed by the global crisis is likely to be based on a misunderstanding of the transmission mechanism. Every major economy that participated in the imbalances will be affected by the crisis, but some countries can postpone the impact of a contraction in global consumption by an expansion in investment, even if that investment turns out subsequently to have been unsustainable. After all, this has happened before, for example to Latin America in the late 1970s. The crisis hit later, but harder.

Reversing the Rebalancing

So was China's reaction to the global crisis appropriate, and more important, did it allow China to avoid a growth slowdown? In his February 17, 2009, testimony at the hearing before the U.S.-China Economic and Security Review Commission, Nicholas R. Lardy, a member of the Peterson Institute for International Economics and one of the most knowledgeable experts on the Chinese economy, famously called China's response to the crisis the "gold standard":

> I would like to focus my remarks on the actions that China is taking in response to the global downturn and to give an assessment of their likely effects. The key point I would emphasize is that China is the gold standard in terms of its response to the global economic crisis. If you look at the magnitude of what they are doing in several domains, it is very substantial, and among the economies that matter, at least according to the International Monetary Fund (IMF), China's stimulus program relative to the size of its economy is larger than that of any other country including the United States, and I think they may have underestimated what China is doing.[2]

I argued in my own testimony that China had indeed boosted credit-fueled demand with its fiscal response to the crisis, but because most of the resulting credit expansion had gone into investment, and not into consumption, China's contribution to global demand over the medium term was minimal and perhaps even negative. Any decline in the Chinese trade surplus would have more to do with painful foreign adjustments than with domestic rebalancing.[3]

In fact in 2012 Lardy made a very similar point about China's current account adjustment in the four years following the crisis, pointing out that rebalancing within China did not cause the adjustment:

> The argument that China's economy is rebalancing internally seems quite weak. Moreover, the current declines in China's external surpluses are

in large part the result of a weak global economy and a modest appreciation of the renminbi, not fundamental rebalancing. The underlying drivers of the surpluses that emerged during the boom years—negative real interest rates on deposits, cheap credit for business, and subsidised land and input prices—are all still in place. China remains unbalanced internally and its large external surpluses may return once the global economy recovers.[4]

Lardy's positive and my negative reactions to China's 2009 fiscal stimulus diverge partly on the issue of short-term versus long-term impacts within China. Lardy suggests that in spite of worsening the imbalances, Beijing's response was appropriate because without it growth would have collapsed in the short term, and this could have derailed long-term prospects. I argued that it was the wrong policy because it seriously exacerbated domestic debt and consumption imbalances, and that it could have been done very differently with a much lower long-term cost.

How? Although it makes sense to worry about the longer-term social impact of an immediate collapse in growth had Beijing not responded with a large fiscal stimulus, I would have argued that the short-term impact of much slower growth could have been mitigated if in 2009 and 2010 Beijing had responded with a much smaller boost in investment and, at least in part, with a real program of wealth transfer from the state to households in the face of the crisis. In that case GDP growth might have dropped, even to 3 or 4 percent, but with household income and consumption growth declining by much less, perhaps to 5 percent thanks to wealth transfers from the state. This would not have been a social disaster at all (although transferring wealth from the state sector is sure to inflame vested interests and so is likely to be politically difficult).

While there is still active disagreement among economists on the advisability of the 2009–10 stimulus, most economic policymakers and advisors in China now agree that the imbalances have gotten significantly worse since the crisis, and there is a cautious acknowledgment, even in the Chinese press, that the stimulus cannot be replicated. In late May 2012, for example,

Xinhua, the official Chinese news agency, said the stimulus was "unsustainable" and warned the market against expecting another.[5]

More important, and in contrast to some of their more optimistic peers, a rising number of policymakers in Beijing recognize that China has not remained unscathed by the crisis and has at best postponed the impact. For example, in January 2012, Liu Mingkang, former chairman of the China Banking Regulation Commission and a very perceptive observer of the Chinese economy, said to a leading Chinese magazine,

> I've said in the past that this economic crisis will spread from the United States to Europe and finally land in Asia. Now we can see that it's already begun influencing Asia.[6]

Liu, and many others in China, increasingly recognize that growth in China during the past decade required vigorous overconsumption abroad in order to maintain the necessary balance between global savings and investment. But as the rest of the world forcibly raises its savings rate and reduces its investment rate, there is simply no way China can maintain its own high savings rate, especially if it hopes to reduce its investment rate. As the world rebalances, China must rebalance just as dramatically and perhaps even more so.

Some Predictions

So how will the global crisis end, and what kinds of rebalancing will have to take place before each of the world's major economies can be said to have put the global crisis behind it? I propose the following:

1. *The United States is slowly and painfully rebalancing.* The United States entered the crisis suffering from high debt and excessively low savings driven by a number of factors. Of these I stress three. First, as the world's most open economy with an extremely flexible financial system, the U.S. economy was the automatic counterbalance to

underconsumptionist policies abroad. These policies led to excessive savings that had to be exported largely to the United States, as foreign demand was correspondingly imported, with this export coming mainly in the form of central bank purchases of U.S. government bonds. Second, and possibly related to the liquidity generated by the recycling of these large trade imbalances as well as to excessively low interest rates in the United States, surging stock and real estate markets made American households feel wealthier—mistakenly as it turns out—and so they increased consumption more than was justified economically. Third, military adventures abroad have been ruinously expensive and, perhaps like most previous unpopular American wars, were funded by borrowing and money creation rather than by taxes.

All three of these factors seem to be reversing, if painfully, which is why I believe the United States will be the first major economy to emerge from the crisis. As of this writing President Obama is slowly extricating the country from its military adventures, the stock and real estate markets have corrected, and overall debt levels are declining, in part through bankruptcy and foreclosures and in part through a massive improvement in corporate balance sheets. What's more, as trade anger rises in the United States and more steps are taken to intervene in trade, the closing of the U.S. trade deficit will automatically cause a boost in domestic growth and in the domestic savings rate.

In fact should the United States take drastic steps to reduce disposable income relative to GDP, like imposing a consumption tax or much higher income taxes on the wealthy, the positive impact on U.S. unemployment and the U.S. savings rate will be dramatic, although it will also be extremely painful for countries, like China and Japan, that rely on American overconsumption to balance their own underconsumption. This would be mitigated if the proceeds of such taxes were used to fund much-needed infrastructure investment, in which case both American savings and American investment would rise, the United States would adjust more slowly but in a healthier way, and there would be much less pain abroad, especially in China, whose own very difficult adjustment requires a benign external environment.

2. *German growth rates will slow sharply for many years, and German banks will take significant losses.* Most of German growth in the past decade has been a direct result of growing European imbalances. As a necessary consequence of its trade surplus, the German banking system has accumulated substantial claims against the trade deficit countries of Europe. The Dutch economist in the *Foreign Policy* article I cited above claimed that China was responsible for the European crisis, and not Germany, because Germany had not run up central bank reserves the way China did, but this argument of course confuses the balance of payments mechanism.

As we showed in chapter 7 German recycling of the German current account surplus through the banking system is not radically different from Chinese recycling of the Chinese current account surplus through the central bank. Policies that restrain consumption growth must push up the savings rate, and if as a result savings exceed investment, the balance must be recycled. Whether it is recycled through the central bank or though some other financial institution simply reflects domestic institutional arrangements. What matters is that the recycling must occur as a consequence of repressed consumption, and with it the corresponding trade imbalances must emerge both at home and abroad.

By definition peripheral European countries, which have heretofore been running large trade deficits, cannot repay their obligations without running trade surpluses, and if they do so, these will force a sharp corresponding deterioration in Germany's trade balance. This leaves Germany with only two meaningful alternatives. Either Berlin must reverse Germany's surplus by cutting taxes and boosting spending, in which case it will suffer from much slower growth, rising unemployment, and rising debt, or it must write off its claims on peripheral European economies, in which case government debt levels will surge anyway as Berlin backstops the banks.

Historically trade surplus countries are the ones that have suffered the most in the medium and long term from global contractions in demand. I expect that this time around will be no different and that Germany will have a very difficult decade ahead of it as it tries to rebalance its own growth toward domestic consumption. The likelihood that its banks will take huge losses on their European claims, of course, will not make the process easier given that, as I will argue in point 7 below, it is the household sector that is usually on the hook for cleaning up banking crises.

3. *Without a strong form of fiscal union or a reversal of German trade surpluses, much of peripheral Europe will be forced to abandon the euro and to restructure its debt.* The problem facing Spain, Portugal, Italy, Greece, Ireland, and the rest of peripheral Europe is not lack of liquidity but rather a lack of competitivity caused by the huge divergence in costs over the past decade. One way of regaining competitivity is to force wages and prices down over many years of very high unemployment. Because, fortunately, this strategy is not compatible with democratic rule, these countries will eventually choose the only practical other way—to intervene in trade, which probably means to abandon the euro and devalue. Of course this will also mean debt restructuring and debt forgiveness given that their already-excessive debt is denominated in what will be a rising currency.

Not everything that is happening is bad, however. Countries like Spain are putting into place real tax, labor, and business reform that will help them grow once the crisis is put behind, but these measures, unfortunately, cannot regain competitivity by themselves. Ultimately these countries will still have to leave the euro. There is no question that abandoning the euro will be painful, but postponing devaluation and debt restructuring will be more painful because the financial distress process will itself ensure that over the next few years businesses will disinvest, workers will become radicalized, savers will flee, and the political structure will become less stable. The sooner the crisis is resolved the less damage there will be to local economies and the more quickly growth will return.

4. *China has already taken too long to address its domestic imbalances, and it is running out of time.* Economists like to debate whether China will suffer a hard landing or a soft landing, but I expect that it will suffer from, to use Nicholas Lardy's phrase, a long landing, and a very bumpy one at that. Growth rates will jump up and down dramatically during the long landing, but the trend will be sharply down. Beijing so far has been very reluctant to force through an adjustment and rebalancing of its extreme underconsumptionist policies, but rapidly rising debt means that within four or five years it will have no choice. As the economy adjusts, I expect Chinese GDP growth to average 3 percent or less over the decade of adjustment.

But contrary to conventional opinion this is not necessarily a disaster for China. If much slower growth is accompanied by a real shift toward labor-intensive industries and a substantial transfer of assets from the state sector to the household sector, unemployment can remain low and household income can continue growing rapidly— perhaps at 4–5 percent a year. This will help prevent social instability and will ultimately leave the country with a much healthier economy and long-term sustainable growth.

For thirty years Chinese households have done well even while receiving a sharply declining share of a rapidly growing economic pie. The state sector, with its growing share, has done even better because its share of the growing economic pie was itself growing. For the next twenty years, as growth slows substantially, the household share must increase. The implication is not just a rapid reduction in the growth of state wealth, but perhaps even an absolute decline. The problem, as many Chinese intellectuals have pointed out, is likely to be the form in which this transfer of ownership from state to households takes place. Strong vested interests are rigidly opposed to many of the most efficient forms of this transfer, and over the next few years China will have to work out the process.

5. *Japan is still struggling with the legacy of its overinvestment surge in the 1980s.* Unfortunately Japan indicates one of the ways China can mismanage the rebalancing of its economy. Rather than write down bad loans and transfer corporate and state wealth directly to households, perhaps by privatization, which might have resulted in a deeper economic contraction in the early 1990s but would have re-energized the capital allocation process and permitted Japan to grow again, Japan instead chose to do otherwise. It hid losses, kept the cost of capital low in order to prevent bankruptcies, and rebalanced the economy effectively by having the government absorb all the noncollectible debt in the economy. Japanese government debt rose from around 20 percent of GDP in 1990 to over 200 percent today.

This is certainly one way of increasing household and private-sector wealth at the expense of the state, but it is extremely inefficient. As a result, any further Japanese adjustment is hampered by its huge and unrepayable government debt burden, made all the worse given the expected halving of Japan's working population over the next forty years.

In recent years, as Japan's debt burden has become increasingly unmanageable, Tokyo seems to have become more serious about paying it down. The most widely proposed solutions, however—increasing taxes, and especially consumption taxes, and repressing household income growth—will have the unfortunate side effect of forcing up Japan's savings rates (by reducing real disposable household income) and possibly reducing investment. Tokyo, in other words, is implicitly attempting to manage Japan's debt burden by forcing up exports relative to imports in a world that is barely able to absorb existing production as it is.

Will it succeed? Probably not, and if it does, it will do so only at the expense of the rest of the world. Rather than try to return to the old days of wealth transfers from households to the state and corporate sector, which it abandoned after 1990, it must continue building household wealth to power domestic growth, perhaps by privatizing assets to pay down debt.

The Global Impact

6. *If it is managed well, China's eventual rebalancing and much slower growth will be positive for China and the world, although the benefits to the world will not be evenly distributed.* If the transition is not mismanaged it will be positive for China because the end of value-destroying investment and environmental degradation will actually increase Chinese wealth—as opposed to Chinese economic activity—and a much larger share will be passed on to Chinese households.

It will be positive for the world because, contrary to popular perception, China is not currently the engine of world growth. With its huge trade surplus it actually extracts from the world more than its share of what is now the most valuable economic resource in the world—demand. A rebalancing will mean a declining current account surplus and a reduction of its excess claim on world demand. This will be positive for the world.

But not positive for everybody. By shifting from investment to consumption, the demand for nonfood commodities will drop sharply, as will the price of metals and other nonfood commodities. This will be very painful for countries that rely heavily on nonfood commodity exports, like Brazil, Australia, and Peru, but positive for commodity importers. On the other hand food exporters should continue to see rising Chinese demand for food as households increase their wealth and, with it, their consumption of food.

7. *Growth in global demand will remain weak for many years.* Traditionally the cost of a banking crisis is borne directly or indirectly by households. Whether it is in the form of forgone deposits, government

bailouts funded by household taxes, or financial repression, households always foot the bill for banking crises. The massive banking crisis unfolding in Europe as the euro crisis works itself out, the expected surge in Chinese nonperforming loans, the 2007–9 bailout of the U.S. banking system, and the costs associated with the still unresolved Japanese banking crisis of the 1980s all imply that households in the world's leading economies will spend the next several years effectively paying for the cleaning up of their national banking systems, in which case it is unreasonable to expect any significant increase in consumer demand over the next few years. The growth in their disposable income will be insufficient to spur a consumption boom.

But it gets worse. Since 2009, the impact on global demand of the sharp drop in global consumption growth was partially mitigated by a surge in investment in China and other developing countries. But the purpose of investment today is to serve consumption tomorrow, and without a revival of consumption, the current surge in investment must itself be reversed. This suggests that overall growth in private-sector demand over the next few years is likely to be minimal.

8. *Trade tensions will rise.* In a world of deficient demand and excess savings, every country will try to acquire a greater share of global demand by exporting savings. This will be called trade protection, currency war, local content requirements, tariffs, and many other things, but these all amount to the same thing. It will be an attempt by each country to gain a greater share of global demand.

The problem may be that the balance of power in trade war rests clearly with one side while the popular perception has it resting on the other side, and this can cause each side to exert more pressure on the other than can be justified. Trade surplus countries often feel that their surpluses rest on unassailable virtues—thrift and hard work—and that because they provide the capital flows that "permit" deficit countries to finance their deficits, they are in a strong position to resist rising protectionism by threatening to revoke credit.

But they are not. Revoking credit is exactly what deficit countries want them to do, whether or not they realize it. In fact it is deficit countries that hold most of the cards. Economists are not supposed to say this because trade intervention is always suboptimal for global growth, but trade war can actually increase employment in diversified economies with large current account deficits. It reduces employment, however, in trade surplus countries. In a world of weak demand growth, demand is the most valuable economic asset. Deficit countries have excess demand and surplus countries are deficient. This is why in most trade conflicts—think of the United States in the 1930s or Japan in the 1990s—the leading surplus countries have eventually suffered the most.

The evidence for the contrary is also pretty clear. For much of the nineteenth century the United States ran trade deficits and consistently used high tariffs (in the second half of the century, judging by tariffs, the United States was the most trade interventionist major economy in the world) to promote employment and manufacturing growth. Tariffs were also used successfully by the United States even late in the twentieth century, for example in 1973, when "the Nixon administration again devalued the dollar by 10 percent. Trade moved back into surplus, the economy picked up speed, and unemployment declined."[7]

The British experience was similar. Tim Booth's study of British protection in the 1930s strongly suggests that until the United Kingdom gave up on its free trade principles in the late 1920s and early 1930s, it was unable to grow and suffered from high unemployment. After devaluing sterling and raising tariffs, however, Britain's economy turned around and reversed its earlier abysmal performance.[8]

This is not to argue in favor of trade protection—there is little disagreement among economists that a world of free trade increases wealth at a faster pace than otherwise. It is only to point out that historically, during periods of global crisis and demand contraction, international trade always suffers and protectionist tensions always rise, and for the reasons that are rational among the participants in trade.

Because deficit countries do not understand how difficult the adjustment will be for surplus countries, and surplus countries do not understand how vulnerable they are to unilateral action by deficit countries and how limited is their ability to retaliate, it is hard to see how conflict can be avoided. It is especially incumbent on the surplus countries to defuse these tensions, even at the cost of some growth. Unfortunately the historical precedents are not very comforting, and the experience of the United States in the 1930s indicates just how dangerous the arrogance of virtue can be for surplus countries.

9. *The world* will *rebalance*. One way or the other the world must rebalance, and it will. Major imbalances are unsustainable and always eventually reverse, but there are worse ways and better ways they can do so. Large trade surpluses can decline, for example, because exports fall, or they can decline because imports rise. Large trade deficits can contract under conditions of high unemployment, but they can also contract under conditions of low unemployment. Low savings rates can rise with declining household income or with rising household income. Repressed consumption rates can reverse through collapsing growth or through surging consumption. Excessive debt can be resolved by default or by growth.

Any policy that does not clearly result in a reversal of the deep debt, trade, and capital imbalances of the past decade is a policy that cannot be sustained. The goal of policymakers must be to work out what rebalancing requires and then to design and implement the least painful way of getting there. International cooperation, of course, will reduce the pain.

Unfortunately it is not clear that this is what is happening in any of the major economies of the world, in which case the rebalances will reverse, but in possibly disorderly and even more painful ways than necessary. Or, as Lewis Carroll put it,

"Would you tell me, please, which way I ought to go from here?"

"That depends a good deal on where you want to get to," said the Cat.

"I don't much care where—" said Alice.

"Then it doesn't matter which way you go," said the Cat.

"—so long as I get somewhere," Alice added as an explanation.

"Oh, you're sure to do that," said the Cat, "if you only walk long enough."

APPENDIX

Does income inequality lead to unemployment?

I N HIS 2014 STATE OF THE UNION Address President Obama referred several times to the problem of income inequality in the U.S. This has become one of the most widely discussed topics in recent months and years, but while Americans agonize over the subject it is worth noting that income inequality is a global issue, affecting not just the U.S. but also Europe, China, and much of the rest of the world.

The surge in income inequality of the past two decades at least partly explains both the global crisis and why we are far from having left the crisis behind us. For this reason, it makes sense to try to figure out why, and under what conditions, rising income inequality might undermine the economy. The adverse social and political consequences of extreme income inequality are pretty obvious, I think, but the economic consequences can seem a little murkier.

From an economic point of view the income inequality discussion is mainly a discussion about excess savings. Distortions in the savings rates of different countries have driven the great trade and balance-sheet distortions with which we are wrestling today, just as they have in most previous global crises, including those of the 1870s, the 1930s, and the 1970s. Rising income inequality and its impact on consumption and investment are fundamental to understanding this model.

It turns out that it is actually not that hard to work through the economic consequences of rising income inequality. When you introduce into the economy a systematic tendency to force up the savings rate, the economy must respond in what are only a limited number of ways. As I will show, some of these responses require an unsustainable increase in debt, and so are temporary. There are, it turns out, two sustainable responses to a forced increase in the savings rate in one part of the economy. The first is an equivalent increase in productive investment. The second is an increase in unemployment.

Before jumping into the argument I want to start by quoting the remarkable former Federal Reserve Board Chairman (1932–48) Marriner Eccles, who may well have been the most subtle economist of the twentieth century, from his memoir, *Beckoning Frontiers* (1966):

> As mass production has to be accompanied by mass consumption, mass consumption, in turn, implies a distribution of wealth—not of existing wealth, but of wealth as it is currently produced—to provide men with buying power equal to the amount of goods and services offered by the nation's economic machinery. Instead of achieving that kind of distribution, a giant suction pump had by 1929–30 drawn into a few hands an increasing portion of currently produced wealth. This served them as capital accumulations.
>
> But by taking purchasing power out of the hands of mass consumers, the savers denied to themselves the kind of effective demand for their products that would justify a reinvestment of their capital accumulations in new plants. In consequence, as in a poker game where the chips were concentrated in fewer and fewer hands, the other fellows could stay in the game only by borrowing. When their credit ran out, the game stopped.

The key point here is that all other things being equal, rising income inequality forces up the savings rate. The reason for this is pretty well understood: rich people consume a smaller share of their income than do the poor. The consequence of income inequality, Eccles argued, is an imbalance between the current supply of and current demand for goods and services, and this imbalance can only be resolved by a surge in credit or, as I will show later, by rising unemployment.

Rising income inequality reduces total demand. It does so in two ways. First, it directly forces down the consumption share of GDP, and second, it reduces productive investment by reducing, as Eccles says, "the kind of effective demand for their products that would justify a reinvestment of their capital accumulations in new plants."

But—and here is where I will presume to add something new to the historical debate about income inequality and underconsumption—there is another very important form of rising income inequality that also forces up the savings rate in a very similar way, and this has been especially important in the past two decades. A declining household share of GDP has the same net impact as rising income inequality.

We have seen this especially in places like Germany and China during the past decade. In both countries policies were implemented that, in order to spur growth and, with it, employment, effectively transferred income from households to producers of GDP (the state or businesses). These policies are described extensively in this book.

As I discuss in chapter 6, the main form of this transfer, in the case of Germany, was an agreement around fifteen years ago to restrain wage growth. By keeping wage growth lower than productivity and GDP growth, unit labor costs declined in Germany and German workers became more "competitive" in the international markets. This forced up the German savings rate and converted Germany's current account from large deficits in the 1990s to the largest surpluses in the world.

In the case of China there were also restraints on wage growth relative to productivity growth and I discuss these in chapter 4. The suppression of wage growth was not so much a policy choice, I would argue, but a consequence of the huge number of underemployed rural workers in China. There were also at least two other very important transfers. First, China has had an undervalued currency ever since 1994, which acts as a spur to growth in the tradable goods sector by effectively taxing foreign imports (and notice, by the way, that something similar happens in Germany, which also has an "undervalued" euro in relationship to the "overvalued" euro of countries like Spain, Italy, and France). This reduces the real value of household income as a share of GDP.

Second, and most importantly, interest rates in China have been severely repressed during much of this century, perhaps by as much as 5 to 10 percentage points or more. This has acted as a huge transfer from net savers, who are the household sector for the most part, to net borrowers, who consist mainly of manufacturers, infrastructure developers, real estate developers, state-owned enterprises, and government entities.

In both cases, and this is true of other countries, especially if they have large state sectors, one of the consequences of these hidden transfers is that GDP, which is the total production of goods and services, rose faster than household income for many years, meaning that households retained a smaller and smaller share of the total amount of goods and services they produced. Of course as the total share of GDP they retained contracted, it is not a surprise that they also *consumed* an ever-declining share of GDP.

The squeezing of the household sector

Notice how this affects total savings. Even if German or Chinese households kept their savings rates steady (i.e. they consumed and saved the same share of their income as before), their consumption as a share of GDP had to decline in line with the household income share of GDP. Most consumption is household consumption, and so as household consumption declines as a share of GDP, total consumption also tends to decline as a share of GDP, which is just another way of saying that total savings rise as a share of GDP.

This is a point that is often missed. Rising income inequality can have the same impact on savings and consumption as a rising state or business share of GDP. In a country in which the state retains a growing share of GDP, the net impact on savings and consumption is almost identical to that of a country in which income inequality is rising. In both cases consumption tends to decline and savings to rise as a share of GDP.

This tendency for rising income inequality, or a rising state share of GDP, to force up the savings rate can be a good thing. If there is a large amount of productive investment that needs to be funded, and not enough savings to fund this investment, increasing the savings rate can cause an equivalent increase in productive investment, and this increase can create sustainable demand for new jobs. Many developing countries have had insufficiently high levels of investment largely because domestic savings were insufficient. By forcing up the savings rate, it was possible to increase investment, thereby creating new jobs.

Notice that these new jobs force up the total amount of goods and services produced, so that ordinary workers will see their income increase even as income inequality increases. The rich will do very well, but the rest will do pretty well too. This process, in short, is the essence of "trickle-down" theory.

But what happens if there is already enough savings to fund productive investment? In that case the impact of rising income inequality is very different. To understand why, let us assume a closed economy with a moderate amount of unemployment (until we begin interplanetary trading the world is a closed economy). We can define the total amount of goods and services produced, which we usually refer to as GDP, in two ways.

First, everything that we produce must be absorbed, and the two ways we can absorb it is either by consuming the goods and services we produce, or by investing them today for future consumption. GDP, in other words, is the sum of everything we either consume or invest, or to put it arithmetically:

GDP = Total consumption + Total investment

This is true by definition. Second, because our total income is equal by definition to the sum of all the goods and services we produce, and there are only two things we can do with our income, consume it today or save it for future consumption, GDP is also by definition the sum of savings and consumption, or, to put it arithmetically:

GDP = Total consumption + Total savings

From these two equations it is obvious that in any closed economy savings is always equal to investment. This simple truth, which is true by definition, has very powerful implications.

Let us assume now that something has happened that caused a transfer of wealth in our economy from the poor to the rich, or that caused the household share of income to drop. To make things simpler we will assume that this transfer occurred without changing GDP, so that the total amount of goods and services is unchanged, but now ordinary households retain a smaller share. This transfer of wealth must have an impact on both total savings and total consumption.

At first the impact might seem obvious. Total consumption will decline and total savings will rise.

But it is not that obvious. In order to maintain the balance expressed in the two equations, mainly the requirement that savings is always exactly equal to investment, something else must happen. There are only two possible things that can maintain the balance:

1. Investment must rise in line with the increase in savings.
2. Savings in fact do not rise, which implies that any increase in savings caused by the transfer of wealth was matched by some other event that caused an equivalent reduction in savings.

I apologize if these sound obvious, but I want to keep the flow of the argument as logical as possible, and so I hope each step follows obviously from the prior step.

Let's take the first condition. Will investment rise? There are, again to be terribly obvious, only three ways investment can rise.

1. There can be an increase in productive investment.
2. Unproductive investment can rise in the form of unwanted inventories.
3. Other forms of unproductive investment can rise.

What causes investment to rise?

Let's consider each of these three in turn before we consider our second possibility, that savings in fact do not rise.

1. There can be an increase in productive investment.

This is obviously the best-case scenario. The tendency to increase the savings rate is met by an increase in productive investment that exactly matches the reduction in consumption. The combination of an increase in productive investment and a reduction in consumption keeps total demand constant, so that there is no imbalance (in the aggregate, of course) between the total demand for and the total supply of goods and services produced by the economy. Because the increase in investment is productive, however, over time the total amount of goods and services produced by the economy will grow, and, presumably, households will be able to increase their consumption in the future.

How likely is this to be happening in the current environment? It is probably not very likely. It is hard to believe that in rich countries, like the U.S., there are a lot of productive investments that are neglected simply because there is an insufficient amount of savings to fund them. I am not saying that every productive investment in the U.S. has already been made, but just that if there are productive investments that remain unfunded, it isn't because of insufficient savings. It might be because of political gridlock, high levels of uncertainty, or something else. Of course it could also be because interest rates are too high, in which case rising income inequality would, presumably by increasing the total amount of savings, cause interest rates to drop. In that case there might indeed be an increase in total productive investment.

But here is where we run into the problem signaled by Eccles. Because the purpose of investment today is to increase consumption tomorrow, if the increase in income inequality is expected to be permanent, the desired amount of productive investment is actually likely to decline. This is because, to quote Eccles again, lower expected consumption would reduce "the kind of effective demand for their products that would justify a reinvestment of their capital accumulations in new plants."

2. Unproductive investment can rise in the form of unwanted inventories.

This, as I understand it, is the process Keynes eventually described after his famous 1930 debate with Ralph Hawtrey. The process is quite easy to explain. As income inequality rises, total consumption tends to decline.

Because in this case there is no equivalent increase in productive investment, the economy finds itself producing more goods and services than it can absorb, and the balance piles up as unwanted inventory, which is a form of unproductive investment. Of course manufacturers are unwilling to pile up infinite inventory levels so this process must eventually stop. Rising inventory levels, in other words, can only be a temporary counterbalance to rising income inequality.

3. Other forms of unproductive investment can rise.

The third way for investment to rise is if the additional savings are used to fund other forms of unproductive investment. Perhaps the tendency for savings to rise without an equivalent increase in productive investment forces down interest rates, with suddenly-cheap capital leading to speculative behavior.

In this case, what Charles Arthue Conant (quoted in chapter 1) called "congested" capital would end up in speculative investments that were not productive—vast tracts of empty apartment buildings, or spectacular but mostly empty airports, railroad lines, super highways and other infrastructure, or increases in manufacturing capacity even in industries that are experiencing overcapacity, or perhaps in a very expensive sporting event—but would nonetheless seem individually profitable because of the expectation that asset prices would continue to rise. These investments, whose low productivity will result in debt rising faster than debt-servicing capacity, can go on for many years, to the point where the implicit losses would have to be recognized, but this is clearly not a sustainable solution to excess savings because it requires limitless debt capacity.

Needless to say this seems to have been a pretty good description of recent investments in places as far apart as Arizona housing tracts, Dublin apartments, extravagant but unused Spanish airports, or Chinese ghost cities and solar manufacturers. We have seen a lot of this before the global crisis of 2007–08, and the seemingly obvious conclusion is that the tendency to increase the savings rate beyond the productive needs of the economy was balanced at least in part by a surge in speculative and unproductive investments.

These three are, logically, the only three ways we can balance the tendency for an increase in savings to be matched with a corresponding increase in investment. Either productive investment rises because productive investment had been constrained by insufficient savings, or unproductive investment rises, either in the form of unwanted inventory or in another form. The first is our best-case scenario, although for the reasons I have noted it is unlikely to describe conditions today, especially in capital-rich countries like the U.S. The second and third ways are unsustainable because they actually destroy value by increasing debt faster than they increase debt-servicing capacity.

What prevents savings from rising?

I said, however, that there is a second perfectly obvious way we can maintain the balance between savings and investments even if there is a substantial wealth transfer from ordinary households (either to the rich, or to the state sector). It is possible that total savings in fact do not rise, which implies that any increase in savings caused by the transfer of wealth was matched by some other event that caused an equivalent reduction in savings.

As far as I can work out there are only three ways a transfer of wealth is consistent with no change in the total savings and consumption shares of GDP.

1. The wealthy or the state consume as much as ordinary households.
2. Ordinary households increase their consumption rate and reduce their savings rate.
3. Unemployment rises.

Again, let us consider each of the three so that we can list the possible outcomes.

1. The wealthy or the state consume as much as ordinary households.

Clearly this hasn't happened and is unlikely to happen in the future. Both common sense and all historical precedent suggest that within any economic entity consumption does not rise linearly with income and households consume a far greater share of their income than the state or business sectors can.

2. Ordinary households increase their consumption rate and reduce their savings rate.

This, which is what happened in the United States and peripheral Europe, is one of those brutally obvious points that so many commentators and economists have failed to grasp. I think the mechanism is fairly easy to understand and has already been much discussed, for example well over 100 years ago by British economist John Hobson who showed how rising income inequality can cause both higher savings and lower opportunities for productive investment. The difference, he argued, poured into speculative stock, bond, and real estate markets or was exported abroad to finance foreign demand for home products.

As money poured into stock, bond, and real estate markets, either at home or abroad, it caused these markets to soar, making everyone feel richer. The consequence was that although ordinary households saw their share of total GDP decline, rising asset prices nonetheless made them feel wealthier and encouraged them to maintain or increase their consumption.

Higher savings generated by the rich or the state, in other words, were matched by lower savings (or rising debt, which is the same thing) among ordinary households. Of course this can only be sustained if asset prices rise forever, but assets are locked into a circular process in which rising asset prices cause rising demand and rising demand justifies higher asset prices.

It takes rising debt to combine the two processes, so it is only a question of time before we reach debt capacity constraints after which the system has to reverse itself, which it did in the developed world as a consequence of the 2007–08 crisis. This process, in other words, is the default reaction to a forced increase in the savings rate in one part of the economy, but it is not sustainable because it requires a permanent rise in consumer debt.

3. Unemployment rises.

There is another way you can force down the savings rate, and this is by closing down factories and firing workers. As workers are fired, their income drops to zero. Their consumption, however, cannot drop to zero, and so they dip into their savings, borrow from friends and relatives, receive unemployment compensation, or otherwise find ways to maintain at least some minimum level of consumption (crime, perhaps, or remittances).

Of course savings is just GDP minus consumption, and so as their production of goods and services drops relative to their consumption, by definition the national savings rate declines. This balances out the higher savings generated by rising income inequality.

To sum up, if the savings rate in one part of the economy rises, without an equivalent rise in investment the only way for the economy to balance is for savings elsewhere to decline, and this can happen either in the form of a (usually credit-backed) consumption binge, or in the form of rising unemployment. The first is unsustainable.

Once we understand this it is pretty easy to explain much of what has happened in the global economy over the past decade or two. As an aside, it may seem strange to many to think that excess savings is not a good thing. We are used to thinking of thrift as good for us, and even more thrift as better, and this belief is embedded with so much moral certainty that we react with repugnance to anyone who suggests otherwise. Bernard Mandeville's *Fable of the Bees* was famously hated in the early eighteenth century for presenting the "un-Christian" claim that spending by the rich was good for the poor and if we all saved everything we would all be destitute, and John Hobson, in his memoirs, tells how his teaching assignment was rejected because of

> the intervention of an Economic Professor who had read my book and considered it as equivalent in rationality to an attempt to prove the flatness of the earth. How could there be any limit to the amount of useful saving when every item of saving went to increase the capital structure and the fund for paying wages? Sound economists could not fail to view with horror an argument which sought to check the source of all industrial progress.[1]

But excess thrift is a much more serious problem than insufficient thrift. There are two reasons besides moral outrage why we get confused about the value of savings. First, and obviously, because more savings is good for individuals, we assume that it must be good for society. It shouldn't take long to see why this is simply wrong.

Second, most contemporary economic thinking is implicitly about the U.S. or the UK (most economic theory comes from economists who have been trained in one or the other country). Because these countries have had a problem in the past several decades with excessive consumption and insufficient savings, we assume that these are universal problems. We want global savings to rise because we want U.S. savings to rise, because what is good for the U.S. must be good for the world. This isn't necessarily true, however.

The global imbalances

Before using this model to examine recent history I think it would be useful to summarize. If the savings rate rises in any part of a closed economic entity, like the global economy, it must be counterbalanced by at least one other change that allows the savings and investment balance to be maintained. Either the investment rate rises, in the form of productive or unproductive investment, or the overall savings rate does not rise because it declines in some other part of the economy.

We are left with the table below that shows the six ways that an increase in savings caused by rising income inequality or a rising state share of GDP must be counterbalanced. Each counterbalance is shown to be sustainable or unsustainable.

Counterbalance	Condition	Sustainability
Increase in productive investment	This might happen if total desired investment had been constrained by insufficient savings.	Sustainable
Rising inventories	If factories maintain production even as sales decline, inventories will automatically rise.	Not sustainable
Increase in speculative investment	If there is excess capital beyond productive investment, it will flow into non-productive investments.	Not sustainable
Linear change in consumption	If consumption rises with income, income inequality need not create a demand shortfall.	Sustainable but a seemingly impossible outcome
Increase in credit-financed consumption	If households feel wealthier thanks to rising asset prices, they will embark on a consumption binge funded eventually by debt.	Not sustainable
Increase in unemployment	If production of goods and services exceeds the demand, factories will fire workers until supply and demand once again balance.	Sustainable

From this table the problem of income inequality is obvious. There are only two sustainable solutions to the problem of a structural increase in the savings rate. Either we must see an increase in productive investment—which is unlikely except in specific cases in which desired productive investment has been constrained by lack of capital—or we must see an increase in unemployment. Nothing else is sustainable.

There are intermediate steps, but because these require debt to grow faster than debt-servicing capacity, they can only continue until debt levels are so high that the market becomes unwilling to allow them to continue to rise. These intermediate steps are easy to understand. At first, in order to keep unemployment from rising, the excess savings can fund a surge in speculative investment or a surge in consumption, or both, with the latter kicked off by the wealth effect that is often a consequence of a surge in speculative investment.

This is exactly what seems to have happened to the global economy. As savings were forced up structurally, whether because of rising income inequality or a declining household share of GDP, the system responded in ways that were sustainable (increases in productive investment) and in ways that were unsustainable (rising inventory in China, increases in speculative investment in the U.S., China, and Europe, and increases in credit-financed consumption in the U.S. and southern Europe). At some point excessive debt eliminated all the unsustainable ways, and we were forced into accepting the remaining sustainable way, which is an increase in unemployment.

I should add here that this model does not tell us where the increase in unemployment must occur, but history tells us much of what we need to know. In the early stages of the adjustment, unemployment usually occurs in the countries that saw the fastest increase in debt, typically the countries with excessively low savings. But as these countries begin to intervene directly or indirectly in trade, the unemployment shifts to the countries with structurally high savings rates—Germany and China, in the current case.

This shouldn't surprise us. As I discuss in chapter 7, if the global problem is insufficient demand, countries that have excess demand (deficit countries) can increase their share of demand simply by intervening in trade. Countries with excess supply (the surplus countries) have to hope that they are allowed to continue to force their excess savings and excess production onto the rest of the world or else their own supply and demand cannot balance.

It is easiest to see this process in Europe. Following the convention I have used throughout this book, I will simplify things by assuming that Europe consists of only two countries, Germany and Spain. Here, as I see it, is the sequence, which is more fully described in chapter 6:

1. Beginning around the turn of the century, and in order to increase German employment, German labor unions, corporations, and the government agreed voluntarily to restrain wage increases in order to make Germany more competitive in the international market. This had a double effect. First, the household share of income declined. Second, as unit labor costs dropped, German *rentiers* and business owners saw their share of total income rise. The net effect was that the share of GDP retained by ordinary German households declined partly because non-households (businesses and the state) retained a growing share of total income and partly because within the household sector the rich retained a growing share.

2. Both effects caused consumption to decline as a share of GDP, or, to put it another way, caused the German savings rate to rise (and notice this had nothing to do with changes in the thriftiness of German households). Higher German savings had to be counterbalanced, either within Germany or within Spain.

3. They were not balanced within Germany. German investment rates did not rise to match the increase in savings (in fact I think investment actually declined), nor did consumption among ordinary German households surge.

If Germany had been a closed economy, a rise in unemployment would have been, in that case, inevitable. Instead, Germany exported the excess savings to Spain, which, under the conditions of the euro, Spain was not easily able to reject (tariffs or currency depreciation being ruled out). Because capital exports are just the obverse of a current account surplus, this meant that after spending much of the 1990s in deficit, Germany's excess production, caused not by a surge in production but rather a decline in consumption, was resolved by the country's running a current account surplus.

4. This resolved Germany's problem, but only by forcing the savings and production imbalances onto Spain. Because savings exceeded investment in Germany, investment had to exceed savings in Spain.

This meant either that productive and unproductive investment in Spain had to increase, or that savings had to decline. The expansion in Germany's tradable goods sector forced an equivalent contraction in Spain's tradable goods sector, so that in order to prevent unemployment (temporarily, as it turned out) Spain had to embrace cheap capital, which unleashed both a speculative investment boom and a consumption boom.

5. And both happened. There was some increase in Spain's productive investment, but the lowering of Germany's unit labor costs relative to Spain made the Spanish tradable goods sector uncompetitive, reducing desired investment in the tradable goods sector. It was difficult, in other words, for productive investment in Spain to rise enough to account for the surge in German savings.

6. As asset prices in Spain soared, thanks to the surge in capital inflows, this made Spaniards feel wealthier. There were two obvious consequences of soaring asset prices. Excessively cheap and easily available money poured into non-productive investments—empty apartment buildings and bloated infrastructure, for the most part. It also funded a consumption binge, and the Spanish savings rate dropped sharply.

7. But neither of these is sustainable. The debt backing unproductive investment and soaring consumption could only continue if there

was unlimited debt capacity. Clearly there was a limit to the debt, and the global crisis in 2007–08 put an end to the party.

8. This exhausted all the ways an increase in German savings could balance save one—a rise in unemployment. Not surprisingly, unemployment soared almost immediately, but of course it did so in Spain. If Spain leaves the euro, Spanish unemployment will decline sharply, but total unemployment will not, which means that German unemployment will rise.

I apologize for being so repetitive, but I want to show as clearly as I can how distortions in the savings rates in one part of the global economy can, in a fairly automatic way, work themselves into the rest of the world through the current and capital accounts.

The Fable of the Bees

Where does this leave us? Until we see a significant downward redistribution of income in Germany, we don't have many options. If Spain were to leave the euro, this would solve its unemployment problem, but only by forcing unemployment back onto Germany.

Many analysts have argued that Spain could have done the same things that Germany did over the past fifteen years and so would not have suffered, but I hope this analysis shows why this solution—so called "austerity"—is completely wrong. If Spain had also taken steps to force up its savings rate by cutting wages, it would only force up the global savings rates even further and, with it, once debt capacity constraints were reached, unemployment, perhaps not in Spain, but elsewhere. The solution to excess savings, in other words, is not for low-saving countries to cut back on consumption. This will only increase global unemployment. High savings countries must increase consumption.

What is very clear from this analysis is that there are really only three sustainable solutions to the global crisis in demand. First, the world can embark on a surge in productive investment, probably but not necessarily directed by the state because the private sector might not be in a position to capture the full benefits of investment and so will not have the incentive to invest. Second, we must reduce the income share of the state and of the rich. Or third, we must accept that unemployment will stay high for many more years. There are no other solutions.

The first solution is possible, but with so much excess manufacturing capacity and excess infrastructure in many parts of the world and with significant debt constraints, we need to be very careful about how we do this. Certainly countries like the United States, India, and Brazil lack sufficient infrastructure, but they do so largely because of political constraints, and it is unreasonable to assume that any of these countries will soon embark on an infrastructure-building boom.

Even if they do, the amount of excess savings is likely to be huge, and without a significant redistribution of income to the middle classes and the poor, it is hard to see how we can avoid high global unemployment for many more years. Because trade war is the form in which countries assign global unemployment, I would expect trade relations to continue to be very difficult over the next few years, as countries with high unemployment and low savings intervene in trade, thus forcing the savings back into countries with excess savings.

So what are the policy implications? Clearly Europe, the U.S., China, Japan, and the rest of the world must take steps to reduce income inequality. Just as clearly countries like China and Germany must take steps to force up the household income share of GDP (in fact polices aimed at doing this are at the heart of the Third Plenum reform proposals in China[2]). Because it will be almost impossible to do these quickly, as a stopgap countries with productive investment opportunities must seize the initiative in a global New Deal to keep demand high as the structural distortions that force up the global savings rate are worked out.

But redistributing income downwards is easier said than done in a globalized world, especially one in which countries are competing to drive down wages. The first major economy to attempt to redistribute income will certainly see a surge in consumption, but this surge in consumption will not necessarily result in a commensurate surge in employment and growth. Much of this increased consumption will simply bleed abroad, and with it the increase in employment.

Less global trade, in other words, will create both the domestic traction and the domestic incentives to redistribute income. In a globalized world, it is much safer to "beggar down" the global economy than to raise domestic demand, and so I expect that there will continue to be downward pressure on international trade.

Until we understand this do not expect the global crisis to end anytime soon, except perhaps temporarily with a new surge in credit-fueled consumption in the U.S. (which will cause the trade deficit to worsen) and more wasted investment in China (which, because it is financed with cheap debt that comes at the expense of the household sector, may simply increase investment at the expense of consumption). These will only make the underlying imbalances worse. To do better we must revive the old underconsumption debate and learn again how policy distortions can force up the savings rate to dangerous levels, and we may have to temporarily reverse the course of globalization.

I will again quote Mariner Eccles, from his 1933 testimony to Congress, in which he was himself quoting with approval an unidentified economist, probably William Trufant Foster.[3] In his testimony he said:

> It is utterly impossible, as this country has demonstrated again and again, for the rich to save as much as they have been trying to save, and save anything that is worth saving. They can save idle factories and useless railroad coaches; they can save empty office buildings and closed banks; they can save paper evidences of foreign loans; but as a class they cannot save anything that is worth saving, above and beyond the amount that is made profitable by the increase of consumer buying.
>
> It is for the interests of the well-to-do—to protect them from the results of their own folly—that we should take from them a sufficient

amount of their surplus to enable consumers to consume and business to operate at a profit. This is not "soaking the rich"; it is saving the rich. Incidentally, it is the only way to assure them the serenity and security which they do not have at the present moment.

NOTES

Chapter One: Trade Imbalances and the Global Financial Crisis

1. Hyman Minsky, *Can "It" Happen Again: Essays on Instability and Finance*, M.E. Sharpe, 1982, 118.

2. See, for example, Charles Kindleberger, *Financial History of Western Europe*, Oxford University Press, 1993.

3. Niall Ferguson, *High Financier: The Lives and Time of Siegmund Warburg*, Penguin, 2000, 16.

4. Charles Arthur Conant, *The United States in the Orient: the Nature of the Economic Problem*, Houghton Mifflin, 1900, 16.

5. Kenneth Austin, "Communist China's Capitalism: The Highest Stage of Capitalist Imperialism," *World Economics*, vol. 12, no. 1, 2011, 79–94.

6. In most textbooks we learn that the sum of the capital account, the current account, and the change in central bank reserves must equal zero, but of course the change in central bank reserves is simply part of the capital account, but segregated for purposes of analysis.

7. Kishore Mahbubani, *Can Asians Think?*, Times Books, 1998.

Chapter Two: How Does Trade Intervention Work?

1. To be technical, we are not really talking about the trade deficit but rather about the current account deficit. The net inflow of capital to Fredonia is equal to the current account deficit, and not the trade deficit. I am not distinguishing between the two accounts for two reasons. First, for most counties the bulk of the current account is the trade account, and so it is really changes in the trade account that matter. Second, this simplification makes an explanation much easier without in any way affecting its correctness. For the rest of this chapter we will assume that the current account is nothing more than the trade account.

2. An increase in exports relative to imports—a narrowing trade deficit or a widening trade surplus—is usually referred to as an "improvement" in the trade account, while its opposite is referred to as a "deterioration." These are mercantilist terms that assume that the former is always good and the latter always bad, when in reality neither is good or bad except under specific conditions.

3. John Ross, "Bogus Arguments for RMB Revaluation," November 27, 2009, China.org.cn.

4.   At the time of this writing, total central bank reserves at the People's Bank of China stood at roughly $3.2 trillion.

5.   This seemingly surprising statement is actually widely accepted by China-based economists. And why not? As of this writing the renminbi has revalued by roughly 30 percent since July 2005, which means that the value of its local currency liabilities has gone up by 30 percent relative to value of its foreign currency assets.

6.   Keith B. Richburg, "China Hopes Social Safety Net Will Push Its Citizens to Consume More, Save Less," *Washington Post*, July 14, 2010.

7.   Justin Yifu Lin, "China and the Global Economy," remarks at the twentieth anniversary of the University of Science and Technology, Hong Kong, March 23, 2011.

Chapter Three: The Many Forms of Trade Intervention

1.   David Pilling, "Where Wukan Has Led Beijing Will Not Follow," *Financial Times*, February 8, 2012.

2.   Carmen M. Reinhart, Jacob F. Kierkegaard, and M. Belen Sbrancia, "Financial Repression Redux," *Finance & Development*, vol. 48, no. 1, June 2011.

3.   Malhar Nabar, "Targets, Interest Rates, and Household Saving in Urban China," IMF Working Paper 11/223, 1.

4.   Jake van der Kamp, "Home Truths about Trade with China," *South China Morning Post*, February 16, 2012.

Chapter Four: The Case of Unbalanced Growth in China

1.   "Premier Wen Jiabao's Press Conference of 2007/03/17," Ministry of Foreign Affairs of the People's Republic of China, www.fmprc.gov.cn/eng/zxxx/t304313.htm.

2.   Andrew Browne, "Beijing Economist Laments Folly of China Planning," *Wall Street Journal*, September 15, 2011.

3.   It is worth noting that because the wealthy consume a smaller share of their income than others, if there is indeed hidden income, and if this accrues mostly to the wealthy, China's savings rate may be even higher, and its consumption rate even lower, than the official numbers.

4.   Yasheng Huang, "Chinomics: The Fallacy of the Beijing Consensus," *Wall Street Journal*, June 19, 2010.

5.   If capital is indeed being misallocated and wasted in China, it should show up in the form of rising nonperforming loans, in which realized losses would effectively reduce GDP growth by the amount of the write-off. Because rather than recognizing

nonperforming loans the banking system resolves them by continuous debt forgiveness as the loans are rolled over at artificially low interest rates, these losses are simply postponed into the future and GDP growth is not adjusted to the lower number. I estimate that this results in GDP growth overstated by at least two or three percentage points annually.

6. Alexander Gerschenkron, *Economic Backwardness in Historical Perspective: A Book of Essays*, Belknap, 1962.

7. Albert Fishlow, "Review of Economic Backwardness in Historical Perspective," February 13, 2003, EH.net.

8. A mainland think tank, Unirule, estimated in 2011 that monopoly pricing and direct subsidies may have accounted for as much as 150 percent or more of total profitability in the state-owned sector over the past decade. Repressed interest rates may have accounted for another 400 to 500 percent of total profitability over this period. Monopoly pricing, direct subsidies, and repressed interest rates all represent transfers from the household sector.

9. Artificially lowering a coupon on a ten-year loan by 4 percentage points represents debt forgiveness equal to 25 percent of the loan. Lowering the coupon by 6 percentage points represents forgiveness of 35 percent of the loan. Although most bank loans in China have maturities of less than ten years, these loans are rarely repaid and are instead rolled over for very long periods of time, thus increasing the value of the implicit debt forgiveness.

10. The German experience, of course, ended in war, and not in a debt crisis, but according to Yale historian Adam Tooze, the German invasion of Eastern Europe occurred three or four years earlier than the military command was prepared for largely because the country was almost insolvent and could not afford to wait any longer. See Adam Tooze, *The Wages of Destruction: The Making and Breaking of the Nazi Economy*, Allen Lane, 2006.

11. The role of nonperforming loans in helping to create China's consumption imbalances is both crucially important and poorly understood. A decade ago Chinese banks, after a post-1997 surge in questionable investment, had nonperforming loans that most estimates put as high as 20–40 percent of total loans. Beijing instituted a number of policies to clean up the banks, and these policies are described in a book by Carl Walter and Frasier Howie, *Red Capitalism: The Fragile Financial Foundation of China's Extraordinary Rise*, Wiley, 2012, probably the single best book on China's extraordinarily inefficient banking and financial systems.

My view of the real resolution of China's banking crisis is a little different from that of the authors. As I see it, the loans were slowly written off over a decade, during which time repressed interest rates allowed borrowers to write of as much as 30 to 40 percent of the value of the original loans. Large parts of the losses, in other words, were effectively transferred to households, who *paid* for them in the form of foregone interest, but because these transfers were hidden, the market was able to believe that Chinese banks had simply "grown out" of their problem loan portfolios.

When this hidden debt forgiveness was combined with a very high spread between the lending and deposit rate, also mandated by the People's Bank of China, the banks were guaranteed very high profits, again at the expense of the household sector, that effectively recapitalized them over the decade. It is not a coincidence that household consumption during this process collapsed from 46 percent of GDP in 2000 to 34 percent in 2010—households, after all, were forced to absorb very large banking losses, and this put significant downward pressure on household income growth.

This is why I have been skeptical about Beijing's efforts to raise household consumption growth rates. If China experiences another wave of nonperforming loans, the seeming success of its last bank recapitalization may encourage it to engineer the same set of solutions, which consists of little more than forcing households to absorb the losses. With such an enormous amount of loss to absorb, it is hard to imagine how disposable household income could possibly rise fast enough to fuel a consumption surge.

12.   For a very worrying look into how that process might occur, see Akio Mikuni and R. Taggart Murphy, *Japan's Policy Trap: Dollars, Deflation, and the Crisis of Japanese Finance*, Brookings Institution, 2002.

13.   Van der Kamp, "Home Truths about Trade with China."

Chapter Five: The Other Side of the Imbalances

1.   It is worth reminding readers that this is not technically correct. It is the *current account*, not the *trade account*, that must equal the gap between savings and investment, but because the trade account is the bulk of the current account, and it is typically what adjusts when the gap between savings and investment is forced to make a major adjustment, it is much easier simply to assume that the current account surplus is nothing more than the trade surplus. This simplifying assumption in no way invalidates the argument in this book.

2.   Remember that the European subsidies paid to Airbus will have probably come directly or indirectly from European households. In that case an increase in European production will be met with a decline, or a smaller increase (it depends on European unemployment levels), in disposable household income and in European consumption. So Europe's savings rate will have automatically risen as Europeans are forced to reduce their consumption.

3.   Ben Bernanke, "Global Imbalances: Links to Financial and Economic Stability," delivered to the Banque de France Financial Stability Review Launch Event, Paris, February 18, 2011.

Chapter Six: The Case of Europe

1.   See, for example, Joseph Cotterill, "There Are Official Creditors and There Are 'Official' Creditors," *FT.com/Alphaville*, January 25, 2012.

2.   Beth Simmons, *Who Adjusts? Domestic Sources of Foreign Economic Policy during the Interwar Years*, Princeton University Press, 1994, 4.

3.   Ibid., 31.

4.   From Herbert Feis, *The Diplomacy of the Dollar: First Era, 1919–1932*, Johns Hopkins University Press, 1950, 14.

5.   David Harvey, *The Enigma of Capital*, Oxford University Press, 2010.

6.   Quoted in Kenneth Moure, *Managing the Franc Poincaré: Economic Understanding and Political Constraint in French Monetary Policy, 1928–1936*, Cambridge University Press, 1991, 27.

Chapter Seven: Foreign Capital, Go Home!

1.   Dr. Stephen S. Roach, chairman, Morgan Stanley Asia, "China's Role in the Origins of and Response to the Global Recession," transcript of testimony at a hearing before the U.S.-China Economic and Security Review Commission, Washington, D.C., February 17, 2009, http://www.uscc.gov/hearings/2009hearings/transcripts/09_2_17_trans/09_02_17_trans.pdf.

2.   Unless, of course that other country was Greece, Spain, Portugal, Italy, or any of a group of countries facing insolvency. China, perhaps not at all surprising, seems however to be in little hurry to purchase their bonds.

3.   I explain why these kinds of balance sheet structures increase the risk of financial crisis in Michael Pettis, *The Volatility Machine, Emerging Economies and the Threat of Financial Collapse*, Oxford University Press, 2002.

4.   A. P. Thirwall, *Trade, the Balance of Payments and Exchange Rate Policy in Developing Countries*, Edward Elgar, 2003, 45.

5.   John Hobson, *Imperialism: A Study*, Cambridge University Press, 1902.

6.   Vladimir Lenin, "Export of Capital," chap. 7 in *Imperialism, the Highest Stage of Capitalism*, from *Selected Works*, Progress Publishers, 1963.

Chapter Eight: The Exorbitant Burden

1.   Harvey, *Enigma of Capital*, 71.

2.   Ambrose Evans-Pritchard, "Hillary Clinton Pleads with China to Buy US Treasuries as Japan Looks On," *The Telegraph*, February 22, 2009.

3.   There have been some truly extravagant claims about the extent of the exorbitant privilege that accrues to the United States. One of the weirdest was detailed in *Currency Wars*, a rather gothic book by Song Hongbin featuring bizarre logic, dubious history, and a spirited dash of anti-Semitism. The book made the Chinese best-seller lists in 2009 and was widely read and discussed by prominent Chinese economists, bankers, central bankers, and conspiracy theorists. It is still read today, although many Chinese economists are now embarrassed by their earlier enthusiasm for the book.

4.   To be complete, there are at least two other benefits to which commentators often refer. First, currency represents effectively an interest-free loan from the holder to the currency issuer (unlike with dollar bonds issued by the U.S. Treasury Department, you do not earn interest on the dollar bills in your pocket).

This means that to the extent that individuals outside the United States hold cash in the form of U.S. dollars rather than in domestic currency (criminals, travelers, savers who worry about the credibility of their domestic currency), this represents an interest-free loan to the U.S. government. Although this is certainly true, the amount of money saved is pretty small relative to the American economy, and anyway in this case individuals hold the dollars not because they are widely held by central banks but rather because they are extremely liquid, widely recognized and accepted, and credible.

The second benefit to Americans is the psychological fillip that accrues to Americans in the form of national pride. In this case perhaps the global dominance of the dollar provides the same kind of psychological benefits to Americans as the global dominance of American basketball.

5.   Simon Johnson and James Kwak, "Don't Blame China," *Washington Post*, October 6, 2009.

6.   I believe it was Brad Setser, currently at the U.S. Treasury, who first made this argument in his blog *Follow the Money*, which before it closed—I might mention—was one of the most influential and important financial blogs in the world and a model for many others, including mine.

7.   Ben McLannahan, "Japan Willing to Go Alone on Yen," *Financial Times*, February 10, 2012.

8.   Tom Orlik, "China Still Has Yen for Japanese Debt," *Wall Street Journal*, February 10, 2012.

9.   Foreigners don't buy just domestic government bonds. They can often buy a very wide range of other domestic assets. But any asset they purchase frees up local currency for the seller of that asset, which he or she then must put to use. In the end, one way or another all foreign inflows add to the same pool of savings available for government bonds.

10.   Zhou Xiaochuan, "Reform the International Monetary System," People's Bank of China, http://www.pbc.gov.cn/publish/english/956/2009/20091229104425550619706/20091229104425550619706_.html.

11.   *China Financial Markets*, mpettis.com.

12.   Barry Eichengreen, *Golden Fetters: The Gold Standard and the Great Depression, 1919–1939*, Oxford University Press, 1996.

Chapter Nine: When Will the Global Crisis End?

1.   Helen Mees, "How China's Boom Caused the Financial Crisis," *Foreign Policy*, January 2012. As an aside, it is common but nonetheless mistaken to point to rapidly rising Chinese demand for luxury cars, Apple iPhones and iPods, gold and jewelry, and other luxury products, as evidence of a Chinese rebalancing toward consumption.

Historically, however, booming sales in luxury products are more likely to be caused by growing income inequality than by rising living standards. This is certainly the case in China, and it is frustrating how often this obvious point is misunderstood.

2.   Nicholas R. Lardy, "Panel I: The Origins of the Financial Crisis and Link to China," in *China's Role in the Origins of and Response to the Global Recession*, transcript of testimony at a hearing before the U.S.-China Economic and Security Review Commission, Washington, D.C., February 17, 2009.

3.   Michael Pettis, "Panel III: The Effect of the Crisis on the U.S.-China Economic Relationship," in *China's Role in the Origins of and Response to the Global Recession*, transcript of testimony at a hearing before the U.S.-China Economic and Security Review Commission, Washington, D.C., February 17, 2009.

4.   Nicholas R. Lardy, "China's Rebalancing Will Not Be Automatic," *East Asia Forum*, February 22, 2012. Although we disagree on our responses to the fiscal stimulus package, we agree on much else, and I would argue that one of the best descriptions of China's economic imbalances, the role of financial repression, and the problems China will face in adjusting is Nicholas R. Lardy, *Sustaining China's Economic Growth after the Global Financial Crisis*, Peterson Institute, 2012.

5.   Kevin Hamlin, "China Abandons Role of Global Engine as Wen Tempers Stimulus," *Bloomberg News*, June 18, 2012.

6.   Ling Huawei, "Liu Mingkang: Responding to the Challenges of 2012," *Caixing*, January 17, 2012.

7.   Jeffrey A. Frieden, *Global Capitalism: Its Fall and Rise in the Twentieth Century*, Norton, 2006, 342.

8.   Tim Booth, *British Protectionism and the International Economy: Overseas Commercial Policy in the 1930s*, Cambridge University Press, 1992, esp. chaps. 2 and 9.

Appendix: Does Income Inequality Lead to Unemployment?

1. John Hobson, *Confessions of an Economic Heretic*, G. Allen & Unwin Ltd. (1938)

2. See Michael Pettis, *Avoiding the Fall: China's Economic Restructuring*, Carnegie Endowment for International Peace, (2013).

3. Hearings before the Committee on Finance, United States Senate, February 13 to 28, 1933, http://fraser.stlouisfed.org/docs/meltzer/ecctes33.pdf.

INDEX

stability issues (*continued*)
62, 71, 86, 165, 167, 169, 171, 175, 179,
186, 188, 222n4; trade imbalances and,
3, 7
stagnation, 77, 82, 89, 133
Stiglitz, Joseph, 174
stock markets: global crisis policy and,
186; insider trading and, 86; printing more stocks and, 126; risk and,
86; trade intervention and, 50–51, 55,
61–62
subsidies: backwardness and, 90–91;
banks and, 87–88; Brazil and, 81–82,
87; China and, 79, 83–84, 87–89,
92–93, 97–99; Europe and, 128, 220n2;
exorbitant burden and, 156; exports
and, 87; foreign capital and, 143; global
crisis policy and, 184; growth and,
80–81, 84–88; investment and, 80–81;
Japan and, 82; manufacturing and, 48,
80–81, 87–88; monopoly pricing and,
219n8; paying for, 87–89; real estate
and, 81, 87–88; social safety nets and,
88; trade imbalances and, 6, 103–5, 109,
111–12, 220n2; trade impact of, 92–94;
trade intervention and, 32, 48–57,
60–61, 65; transfer consequences and,
55–58; Unirule and, 219n8

Taiwan, 75
Tardieu, Andre, 134–35
tariffs: China and, 112; competition and,
9; countermeasures to, 112; Europe
and, 126; foreign capital and, 136;
global crisis policy and, 192–93;
increasing trade tensions and, 192–94;
trade imbalances and, 9, 14, 26–30,
32, 47–48, 105, 112, 126, 136, 192–93;
mechanisms of, 28; trade intervention
and, 9, 14, 26–30, 32, 47–48, 105, 112,
126, 136, 192–93
taxes: Asian development model and,
82; Brazil and, 81, 87; China and,
83–88, 112; Europe and, 30, 121, 123,
128; exorbitant burden and, 156, 162;

foreign capital and, 137, 146, 148; Germany and, 30, 121, 128; global crisis
policy and, 186–88, 190, 192; growth
and, 84–87; hidden, 47, 55–57, 60,
83, 85–88; Japan and, 82; negative,
84; social safety nets and, 88; Spain
and, 130; subsidies and, 87 (*see also*
subsidies); tariffs and, 9, 14, 26–30, 32,
47–48, 105, 112, 126, 136, 192–93; trade
imbalances and, 15, 112; trade intervention and, 28–32, 45, 47, 53, 55–57,
59–60, 65; undervaluation, 53; value-
added (VAT), 121
technology, 9, 72, 89, 142, 164, 167–68
Thailand, 75
thrift, 160, 192; France and, 135; Germany
and, 13, 119, 127–34; Spain and, 13,
119; trade imbalances and, 13, 20–22,
100–6; trade intervention and, 28, 30,
34, 42, 65
toxic waste, 48–49
trade account: China and, 74, 78, 84,
140–41; Europe and, 140; foreign
capital and, 140–41; imbalances and,
4, 19–20, 220n1; intervention and,
107n2, 217n1; vs. current account,
220n1
trade deficits: China and, 78–79, 93, 98,
100, 136–42, 187; currency manipulation and, 14, 32–34, 47; Europe and,
92–93, 119, 127, 129–30, 133, 143–45,
147, 187; exorbitant burden and, 155,
157, 163–64, 175–76; foreign capital
and, 136–43; France and, 129; global
crisis policy and, 186–87, 193–94;
Greece and, 129; imbalances in, 10–11,
100–8, 111–18; increasing trade tensions
and, 192–94; interventions and, 26–36,
50, 217nn1,2; Italy and, 129; Spain
and, 129, 144–45, 147; United States
and, 92–93, 136–42, 155, 157, 163–64,
175–76, 186, 193
trade imbalances: accounting identity
and, 17–19, 101, 104; banks and, 110, 114,
186; bonds and, 114, 118; capital flow